How to Survive
a Career in
Consulting

John Kumar

To my ex-bosses (both good and bad):

Thank you for the memories!

Part I: Getting In

Understanding the work environment

Before we start talking about getting a job at a consulting firm, it's worth taking a moment to understand the work environment at these firms and what you're actually getting into.

The average age of en employee at these firms is usually in the mid- to late-20s. If you are targeting a Big 4 firm, the average age tends to be around 26 or so, while if you were to look at a white-shoe, boutique consulting firm, the average age there is about 30 or so.

Is this a bad thing? Not necessarily so. It provides a youthful environment to work in and with a fresh intake of employees every year, there's a sea of younger people joining and older ones making their way out. It's not like a typical job at 'industry', which is consultant-speak for clients' offices, where someone joined as a graduate and stayed on for life.

But it's worth keeping the age factor in mind. If you're slightly older, say 40s or older, you would have gotten used to a certain pace of life, both in the office and at home, and coming in to a consulting firm at this stage can be a shock to the system. Not only is the pace of life more intense, but your colleagues are a decade younger than you and you may find yourself reporting to someone who's younger, and possibly less experienced, than you. Worth keeping in mind when you find yourself one day at a fixed cubicle at industry, but then the next day at a consultant's office struggling to find a hot desk and the nearest person who can help you is barely older than your eldest child.

During the course of this book, I won't go into why you should or should not become a consultant. That's for your to decide. But I'll paint a picture of what it's actually like to work at one of these firms and will give you a better idea of what you're getting into before actually biting the bullet.

I worked in a Big 4 firm for close to seven years and am well-placed to speak on the fun and games that go on at such places. Hopefully, my guide will give you the information you need, while entertaining you along the way.

I sometimes describe situations through fictional characters and situations. These are figments of my imagination and bear no resemblance to any person, living and dead, and are used purely for illustration purposes.

What that out of the way, let's move on the first thing about getting a gig in consulting — going for the job interview!

❀ ❀ ❀

Job Interviews

I still remember my interview like it was yesterday. I'd shown up all bright and starry-eyed as a qualified accountant and was looking to move on up in my career. I thought that getting a job at a prestigious consulting firm would do wonders for my career and, truth be told, it did. To this day, I still get calls from recruiters from the industry asking me whether I'd be interested in some banal position or the other at yet another bank or hedge fund.

The first thing to note for the interview is to not show up too early. If you have an interview at 9am, but you arrive before 8:45, go take a walk around the block to get some fresh air and calm your nerves. It's best to arrive around 10 minutes before the interview, 8:50 in this case.

This was perfect timing, as you'll come come to learn on this and at future interviews. It shows that you treat the interview with importance and therefore showed up early, but not too early so as to come across as eager for the job. This may seem like a small thing, but it will be noted by the interviewing team.

You'll usually be interview by two managers, sometimes both at the same rank or, more often than not, one a more senior manager and the other a junior manager. Note, I'm referring to their seniority and not their actual job titles.

The usual pecking order is Associate -> Executive -> Manager -> Senior Manager -> Director -> Executive Director -> Partner. Sometimes, partners (the owners of the business) are further categorised into: partners (meaning junior partners), senior partners and managing partners. The latter is usually in charge of a department or specialised team. A department is called a 'practice' in consultant-speak.

Going back to the job interview, if interviewed by a more senior person, say at partner or director level, prepared to be bored to tears. This person will hog the limelight and using the interview mainly as an opportunity to speak about himself and how he has progressed from the bottom ranks to partner.

However, once the formalities are done and Mr. Windbag has had his 15 minutes of fame, the real interview starts. This means that the first of a series of screwball questions will come your way.

"Tell me about yourself."

Umm, what? Didn't this guy read your CV? Obviously not, as you see his eyes scanning your CV while waiting for your answer. If he had done his homework, he would be waiting expectantly for your response.

I suggest you go into a spiel of how you progressed thus far in your career and why this firm would be a good next step. That seemed like a good enough answer, but you may have more curveballs thrown your way.

"If you were an animal, what kind would you be?"

Don't laugh. This is a very common question at job interviews.

So, here you are for an interview and you land up with the MBA-wannabe who just read a newly-minted manager's guide to interviews.

Reply with something smart, yet equally inoffensive. I suggest saying that you saw yourself as a cheetah, able to chase the gazelle and move at frighteningly quick speeds. You may feel like you sound like an idiot, but hang in there. Their eyes will usually light up and your interviewer will look as if he'd found a soulmate.

If he compliments your response, you may think to yourself, "Huh? Was this guy serious? I thought of some banal response and here he is lapping it up. Maybe he is actually dumber than he looks."

He might be, so try not to burst out laughing.

There'll usually be a follow-up question like, "How many ants are there in an anthill?"

This question is not meant to test numerical accuracy, but how you'd approach a situation that you wouldn't normally expect to.

I would start off by giving him an answer based on lots of assumptions and lots of probabilities. You could say something like, "Well, an anthill is usually about 30 cm high and an ant is about 1/2 a centimetre long. Using that logic, I'd extrapolate that the surface are of the anthill is about 30 cm2 and that 2/3rds of this would be free for ants to live in. Based on that, I reckon the actual number of ants is approximately 2000. In this case, at least."

They're looking to see how quickly you can make assumptions (which will be useful when talking to clients) and how you can run with these assumptions to arrive at conclusions. This is a smaller version of how consultants arrive at solutions for their clients, so the faster you pick up this skill, the farther you'll go in such a job. Or, at least at the job interview.

Don't worry about the numerical accuracy, as long as you're not way off target like saying that there are ten ants in an anthill or something like that. Just walk them through your logic and you'll be fine.

❊ ❊ ❊

If you're successful, you'll get a call later that week and the firm will arrange a second-round interview with a partner. If you pass that round, an offer is usually made.

Naturally, you should turn them down and make some story up of doing other interviews and that their offer is sub-par or underwhelming. If you've come across well in your interviews and have played your cards right, they will come back with a revised offer a week later and you may accept it.

If you're unlucky, you'll get offered a position one below you were applying for. As an example, if you were applying for a Manager's role, you might be offered 'Junior Consultant' or 'Executive' instead. Even though you aced all the interviews, the partner who you'll be ultimately reporting to might be the finicky type. If you have no prior experience in consulting, he may reluctant to put you in charge of projects and of people from the get-go (which is what a Manager will typically deal with). You may think that sounds fair, but take for a moment before deciding.

It is one of the the oldest tricks in the consulting recruiting book. You'll learn that it was common to interview someone for a Manager's role, but then decide that they couldn't meet his pay expectations, yet still wanted him on board their team. So, they pull the old 'not experienced enough' card and offered you a position below.

In any other industry, candidates would laugh their asses off and walk out the door with their dignity intact. Consulting, however, especially in a big-brand, prestigious firm means that the employers have a slight upper hand in such negotiations. There are loads of people desperate to join and a good name on your CV is an almost guaranteed golden parachute into any other job when your time here is done.

So, you'd think that this was a fair deal where you get to join a big firm and they would get someone who would work their way up. Sounds great. Until your first week at work, that is.

That's when you meet your colleagues in the new department and realise that many of them are not from a consulting background either, but were able to hold firm when interviewing and stuck to the Manager title during negotiations. In other words, it was a game of chicken, where you blinked first and lost out.

So beware of not only been screwed over a job title (and higher pay), but also losing out to future colleagues. Colleagues you'll now be reporting to.

That is how to get admitted into the funny farm.

✳ ✳ ✳

Settling In

Let's assume you got made an offer and that you accepted it. Congratulations! Welcome to your new career in consulting.

In your first week in 'the firm' (which is the term everyone uses to refer to the company), you'll usually come across two distinct people. A 'buddy' and a 'counsellor'.

A buddy is someone of the same rank as you, but who has been in the firm for a while. He is there to help you with mundane matters like finding a red stapler or an expense envelope or to help you navigate trickier problems like finding project billing codes or whom to contact in case you get stuck on something. He's there to help ease your transition into the firm and is usually a friendly chap. Still, he's a potential competitor for a future promotion and I'd suggest being friendly yet guarded about what you say to him and what you actually think about the firm. Remember: loose lips sink ships.

The next person you'll come across is arguably the more important one — the counsellor. He (or she) is usually two ranks above you and is for all practical purposes a mentoring manager to help you and your career in the firm. You are, in turn, the counsellee.

This is a staple feature of consulting firms, though when if you were to mention to people outside professional services that you have a counsellor at work, they might think that you have mental health issues. Reassure them that that's not the case.

Everyone at the firm is assigned a counsellor. Everyone. Right from the lowest secretary to the partners, the owners of the business. In many professional services firms, you have this senior colleague who is not your boss, but guides you through the promotion process and, if you're lucky, helps you score the juicy assignments. The assignments that have 'high visibility' among the partners and can either make or break your career.

Sometimes, you get assigned a counsellor who is on the partner fast-track programme. Membership in this programme implied that the partners saw leadership potential in you and wanted to ultimately see you rise up to partner level, the highest in such firms.

Some would say the fast-track scheme is just a ruse to get people all excited, get them to work ever more without complaining and to mould them into the androgynous drones that employees at these firms have begun to epitomise. If nothing else, it is said to breeds haves vs. have-nots in the office and people get ultra-competitive just to get into such cherished programmes. A sort of in-house, by-invitation-only, country club membership, if you will.

I'll leave it up to you to make up your own mind on such schemes and whether you want to put in the extra hours to make it rain in your career.

Choose your counsellor wisely, if you get the choice. Truthfully, you don't have many options as 'firing' your counsellor is a no-no in such firms. It is the equivalent of slapping someone in the face and would not be taken lightly. Funnily enough, all counsellors in consulting firms bang on about 'taking charge of your career', but when it comes to firing your counsellor because he or she is doing a poor job and you want a replacement, then suddenly you are met with hushed silences and admonishments about how you 'need to get along with others' and 'be a team player'. It's amusing how taking charge of your career only applies when you fit their mould and do what they told you to do.

❄ ❄ ❄

Part II: Surviving

(Not) Working

Working life has changed a lot since the 1950s and 1960s. For one, people don't really work with their hands anymore. We're now a service-led economy and factories don't fit in with this picture anymore.

Secondly, almost everything is done on computers these days and so the work takes a fraction of the time it used to before. In the past, an accountant may have taken a couple of days to prepare your income tax statement, but now he just plugs in the numbers on some spreadsheet, fiddles with a few calculations here and there and, hey presto, it has now spit out how much you owe the taxman. Yes, please sit down and take a breather while you work out how to pay the taxman the monstrous sum you now owe.

But most important of all, is that if you look closely, there is not enough work to go around. Look at a consultant's office you're in and the colleagues around you. I'm convinced you'll come away thinking that this is some sort of house of cards that is all going to come crashing down soon. Your department may have some 300 people or so, but don't be surprised if you can't tell if anyone is doing any work.

Whenever you pass by someone's desk, there's always someone whose screen has a minimised browser window with her online shopping there. Or someone using the company phone to arrange for a boiler serviceman to pop around their home.

You'll frequently wonder to yourself, "Is anyone doing anything here at all?!"

Oh sure, you may be able to find the occasional person who's breaking his back on a project and working really hard, but a lot of time spent during the day is unproductive. Colleagues checking their personal email, gossiping to each other on the in-house instant messaging software and people looking for new jobs. You'll see it all.

When at 'home base' (i.e. your office), most 'work' will consist of pointless meetings, useless strategy sessions and boring 'diversity' or 'equality' training programmes.

Most pernicious of all, you have to pretend like you're really busy and that if you didn't make it to work that day, the world would come to an end.

Monday mornings are so predictable that it's almost comical. In a regular industry, ask colleagues what they did over the weekend and you're usually bored to tears with stories of children's birthday parties, BBQs with friends or someone's tale of house-hunting as they need to upgrade after earning their most recent bonus. Maybe the occasional friend's wedding to spice the mix up, if someone was really the adventurous sort.

Come in on a Monday at any consulting or other professional services firm and ask your colleagues what they did and you'd have a predictable set of responses:
1) They were working the whole weekend because the project they're working on is

so important (yet is, inexplicably, running behind schedule!);

2) Tales of playing golf with the partner you report to; or

3) Studying for yet another professional qualification to aim for that next promotion.

In short, as boring as people may seem in the real world, the driods that work in the consulting industry are totally vapid and devoid of any fun. Watching paint dry would be more exciting than spending time with them. The sad truth is that many of these young professionals are either working at the office on the weekends (the small minority of hard workers) or that they spent the weekend at home so tired from wasting 90 hours a week at work that they make up tales to regale and entertain, when in reality their lives are boring and empty.

It wouldn't be so bad if these people were actually working 90 productive hours a week. But since we know the real truth of how most of their time in the office is spent watching videos of dogs chasing their tails, it's tough to take any of them seriously.

What's really amusing is when you step into the lifts on a Monday and the first question people ask is, "What are you working on?"

Not: How are you? How was your weekend? Could we catch up later?

Nope. What are you up to and how can I find some schmuck to join my project, potentially lining him or her up as the fall guy in case things go tits up (which they inevitably do).

Predictably, in order to make it known that you're someone in demand, that you're on top of your game or that you're not too keen to work with said questioner, you come up with even more lame responses.

"Yeah, I'd love to help, but I'm swamped with three projects and have been working flat out 90-hour weeks for a month now. We've been really working hard with Client X to streamline their operational loss model results and to rationalise its results with peer outputs and benchmark them against best practices. I'd love to help, I really would, but I can't take anything on at the moment. But I heard Linda has some availability and she may be able to help. She's usually in by 8:30, so make sure to swing by her desk early before she gets sucked up into someone else's project."

If you really wanted to sweeten the deal, just add, "She's really good, from what I hear."

That's right. It's your number one get-out-of-jail card. If in doubt, pull in the consultant jargon from the management consultant dictionary and dazzle them with meaningless babble, while positioning yourself as someone who apparently knows something. Of course, don't forget to stitch up your colleagues while you're at it as why should you let a good opportunity pass. If you're too polite to do it, I can almost guarantee that Linda will screw you over if she gets the chance. After all, if you don't get that promotion this year, Linda will.

In most other industries, you'd be laughed off as a clown. A snake-oil salesman. A buffoon. A charlatan. A fraud. But not here. Here, you'll make it to partner in no time.

❄ ❄ ❄

And that is where you learn your first lesson. Don't believe what the others say — working hard will not get you anywhere. It's not even about 'working smart', whatever that is supposed to mean. You just have to pretend that you work; in most cases, that's enough to get by around here. Dare I say it, is it different in any other modern workplace?

The biggest trap is when someone, seemingly innocently, asks you to join them for after works drinks at the local watering hole. This is usually asked in front of your colleagues or, worse, the partners.

Whenever anyone asks you a question like that, you should always take a moment to look who's around you and *then* answer the question. If it's some nobody, go ahead and say what you want. But if it's a senior colleague or someone from your department around, you want to make it sound like you're really busy and that you're drowning in work. But, just to be one of the lads, you'll finish up shortly and join them later.

It's 5:30 on a Thursday evening and your colleagues are still here at work. You and I both know that they're doing nothing and probably surfing cat videos on YouTube. But they don't let on. They pretend like they're so busy and that if they don't stay back and work some more, some starving child in Africa will die or something.

So, the next time someone asks you this question, say something like 'Oh yeah, I'm really busy. I got a lot to get through. But I'll try and join you guys later. Just email me your location and I'll pop over if I get a chance.'

Whether you go to the drinks or not is immaterial at this point. But you've made an impression of being a team player and

one who is willing to put himself above
wine and country.

❈ ❈ ❈

Face Time

In the consulting industry, putting in face time is important, both in front of your bosses and in front of clients. The smart consultant will manage his time between both offices, managing to look like he's at two places at any given time.

The smarter consultant — which you, naturally, consider yourself to be — is one who is in neither office and is, for all practical purposes, incommunicado. Instead, you are chilling at home or running a few personal errands. If you've gone the family way, you'll probably want to spend time with your children. Or, just getting some shut eye once the brats have left for school.

The trick is the use the facilities provided to you and exploit them to the maximum. That's another consulting line, in case you missed it.

Consulting firms operate on a very simple business model. They've got people and these people need to be at clients' offices earning the partners money. Bums on office chairs equal no money. Bums on clients' chairs equal big bucks.

So, these firms invest heavily in technology to make sure that they have a 'mobile workforce'. That means lots of Blackberries (or regular mobile phones if you're not important enough), remote computer logging in facilities, a virtual 24-hour IT support desk, a standard-issue laptop for everyone (including partners), large email inboxes and instant messaging platforms (even though they're a total time sink).

Any- and every-thing to make sure that you can work from anywhere in the world, even from home. Sounds good on paper. It gets even better in real life.

What this actually means is that you can be out of sight and, thankfully, out of mind if you know how to play your cards right. Your boss thinks you're working from the client's site and vice versa, while you're actually at home sipping some home-brewed chai on a chilly winter's morning. No one is the wiser, unless you actually need to meet someone face to face.

That might appear to be a problem at first, but consultants have found a way around that as well and have easily solved it. Schedule these meetings either early in the morning or late in the afternoon so that the rest of the day can be spent goofing off. Think this doesn't work? Think again.

When was the last time you saw your consultant actually putting in 60 hours a week at your office, when that's what it says on this week's invoice? Sure, you saw the guy pop into the office this morning for a meeting, but he then disappeared to 'consult with his senior colleagues'. He went missing for the rest of the week, but his invoice promptly lands on your desk, detailing all the 'deliberations' he's had back at home base on your 'tricky problem'. I think I've made my point.

The trick, then, is to send some communication once in a while to indicate that you're still alive. A call to the partner to 'discuss an important client issue' or to 'pick his brain' on some asinine matter leaves him or her assured that you're on the job. A call to your subordinate 'on your way to another client meeting' teaches him not to goof off while you're so hard at work. A strategically placed voicemail to the client's desk phone long after he's caught the 18:20 train to Basingstoke while stuffed under someone's armpit is meant to leave him with the impression that you're burning up the midnight oil in the office reviewing his precious documents.

When you actually have to make an appearance at the office, you might want to pretend that you couldn't find space next to your team and instead hot desk at some random location in some random floor. Maybe there is something to be said about the modern office menace of 'hot desking' after all.

It is all just one big sham and everyone is in on it. Everyone. No one in the consulting industry dare speak about it as, after all, who wants to kill the goose that lays the golden egg? Especially when you've got a wife, three kids and a mistress to provide for. Not to mention the golf club membership, holiday home in southern Spain and sky-high mortgage for that cold mansion in the home counties.

Clients don't speak about it as how else would these perenisally-insecure creatures get that much-sought after seal of approval from their prestigious consulting firm of choice for what is, at best, average work. Who wants to be caught out for being a poor waste of space and for being exposed as not knowing anything at all? Nope. Better to call in the insurance policy and have an external firm vouch for you and your (in)competence. You'll gladly sign that six- or seven-figure cheque to pay their latest invoice. To be cleared within 14 days of receipt, of course.

And moronic members of the media dare not report on it, with the exception of a few brave souls, as who else was going to spend so much money on needless advertisements on your website or, decreasingly, actual printed newspapers. Or, invite them for soirées with all-you-can-drink open bars and more attention lavished on them than from their crabby spouse back home.

No one rocks the boat. Got it? No one.

* * *

Real Life

When you get sold the image of a career in consulting at recruitment fairs, it sounds glamorous. A new city every month — Paris, Berlin, Milan, New York, Hong Kong, Singapore, Tokyo or Sydney. The list is almost limitless. Once they see your eyes light up at such names, the members on the recruiting team know they have you and reel you in.

While the picture of a consultant's life is that of a postcard from every major global city, the reality is far, far different. For one, you're more likely to be sent to Bradford or Hull, rather than the exotic, international locations. Very few cross-border assignments require staff to be imported from another country's office. In addition, the senior staff will pull rank and get themselves on such projects rather than sending a junior peon over.

Couple this with the fact that even if you did get the chance to work in a cool city, you're unlikely to actually enjoy it. You'll most probably be camping at an airport hotel or at one far from the city centre and you'll actually get very little time to see the city. You'll 'work' something like 16 hours a day (as the client's paying to import you) and you'll be so dead beat by the end of the day, that all you'll want to do is order room service and just go to bed.

You'll barely get time to go home for the weekend, but all that time will be taken up running your weekly errands and catching up on lost sleep. You'll barely have time for anything else. When you consider that you'll be travelling back home late on Friday night (reaching home probably sometime after midnight) and that you have to pack your bags again on Sunday night so that you have a fresh Monday morning start, you actually have only a little over a day to spend at home.

So far, it sounds terrible. And it is. But this is only considering the point of view of a single person. You somehow manage to pull it together and move on eventually.

If you're in a relationship, however, you're done for. You're never there for your partner; they have to build a social life without you; when you are there, you're too exhausted to do anything; you're moody and irascible; and, worst of all your sex life dwindles down to non-existent.

Your libido is shot to bits from the stress, long hours at the office, crabby clients and their unreasonable demands, cantankerous colleagues, insufficient sleep and the lack of exercise. In short, any- and every-thing that can interfere with your sex life will happen. Sometimes when you hear how American postal workers go off the deep end and start shooting people, you don't seem that surprised. Tell a bloke to work in consulting at a top-tier professional services firm and he too just might go postal if he had access to a gun.

To make matters worse, you find yourself changing as a person and your partner begins to feel more distant. Maybe you're not the same person they fell in love with and they begin to question if the relationship is worth it.

Inevitably, this job results in a breakdown of relationships, many-a-time an office affair tipping a rocky relationship over the edge. A professional services workplace is littered with inter-cubicle romances, though the participants in such relationships are not always mutually exclusive, nor necessarily single.

❈ ❈ ❈

Many consulting firms are regularly listed in the 'Best Places to Work at' league tables and therefore have a reputation as being a 'women-friendly' and 'gay-friendly'. What this meant is that you get all types here and they tended to stick on for a while, irrespective of competence or intelligence. If you were a 'minority' of any sort (race, gender, sexuality) and joined one of the various minority support groups, you are safe as long as you do not commit gross negligence or violate the law.

Incompetence, bullying, lying and skullduggery would all be tolerated and turned a blind eye to if you are a special snowflake and belong to one of these cabals.

❊ ❊ ❊

Most of the people you'll come across, however, are a mixed bag. One end of the spectrum consisted of partners who had 'made it' but had paid the price of looking twice their age — the stress, long hours and endless consumption of make up, cigarettes and alcohol had ruined their skin, made them put on weight rapidly and made them look as if they had life sucked out of them.

On the other end of the scale, you will come these nubile twenty-somethings joining the firm in droves each year, who essentially knew nothing and seemed happy to stay that way. Many, however, were there just because of their looks and their sense of style. It is tough to expect your clients who paid good money for your services to actually take them seriously, but somehow the clients seem not to mind.

❊ ❊ ❊

That is the case with a lot of colleagues. If you want to be a cut above the rest, I'd recommend taking a different path. While it is all right to be jokey and charming with colleagues at the office socials, Christmas parties and training sessions, try being a different creature when working on projects. I recommend being a guy who is known for doing a good job. And a good job was defined by the client, not necessarily some internal committee.

I recommend pulling out all the stops to get the job done, but within reason. Long hours, weekends and public holidays, cancelling vacations, cancelling personal obligations after work and even pulling in the occasional all-nighter was good for the other guy, but don't do so yourself. Or, at least, not too often. Remember, if they know you're a hard worker, everyone, including the lazy ones, will find a way to dump work on your desk on a Friday night while they're out getting plastered at the local bar.

Consider yourself warned.

❊ ❊ ❊

Culture

It's an early start at these places. The partners like to see everyone at work nice and early as if it were some sort of test of loyalty. If you're there by 7:30 am, you're considered one of the heroes and a 'team player'. Come in before 8:30 and you're a good worker and can be seen as dependable. Come in at 9am or after and they look at you as if you have leprosy and they wonder why they hired you in the first place. They curse their stars for having such bad luck and for hiring such a slacker.

Normally, I wouldn't worry you about such things. However, if performance review season is coming up, you need to be on your best behaviour. You'll realise that every action counts, no matter how small, and so I recommend jumping onto a bus at 7:05 to make it in the office by 7:30. Once you get there, make it a point to talk to some of the partners of how 'busy you are', how 'great the project is going', how the client 'loves the work you're doing', and just about any- and every-thing else to make them believe that you're the best thing to happen to the firm since sliced bread was invented.

Sometimes, when you're having these conversations with your bosses or colleagues, you'll wonder if it's all worth it. You get up everyday to spend your time with less-than-stellar colleagues, trudge through the office hours and end the day so tired that you have no energy to do anything else but crash into bed. Then you remember the promotion you're working for and all the hard work you've put in so far. The end is in sight and you have to work hard just a bit longer. Back to the game, then.

So after the obligatory boast about how great the project is, how you're doing a great job on it and how the client just loves you and the work you're doing, it's time to head off to the client's office so that you can be there for a 9am start.

❀ ❀ ❀

Drink Up

Let's say it's Friday night and you're out drinking with your colleagues. So that means that some other schmuck is burning the midnight oil at the office tonight. Good going! You get an extra life, like in the video games.

If your manager is around, he may open the account, pitch in a £100 tab behind the bar and invite the department for drinks. No one says no to a free drink and so the event will end up being oversubscribed. Somehow, people from other departments will show up and the bar tab runs out pretty quickly.

Free drinks over, people start getting their credit cards out. Nothing will stop drinking in this industry. Alcohol is such an integral a part of work life here. It is a tradition in itself. Those that do not drink up will not really fit in. Many promotions or business deals have been struck at bars rather than back at the cubicle farm or in meeting rooms. Is it any surprise that videoconferencing never took off in a big way? If it doesn't involve alcohol or putting a face to a name over the clinking of beer glasses, it won't take off.

The short lesson here is: drink up. Your long-term career here depends equally on socialising with your moronic colleagues, as much as it does on putting in face time back at the cubicle farm.

❊ ❊ ❊

Knowledge Sharing

One thing you'll come across frequently at consulting firms (and, for that matter, at most other professional services firms) is a lot of 'knowledge-sharing' sessions. These are nothing but presentations that you give to other staff members on what project you're working on, what problems you've encountered, how you handled them and how the client is always happy at the end. These things are so predictable that it's a joke. Everyone and his dog is organising one, as this is a good way to get 'visibility' among the partner group and to show them how you're so great and how everyone else in the firm can learn from you. Don't lose this opportunity to shine as the others you're competing with will usually dismiss it when suggested as 'feedback' from their counsellors. You know, to 'raise their visibility' in the department.

Truth be told, a lot of the feedback you get is a total waste of time. If there's one lesson I can share with anyone else, it'd be this: just do your job and don't screw anything up.

It's that simple, ladies and gentlemen, and that's all there is to it. No rocket science. No fancy management theory. No jazzy jargon. Just good old hard work and keeping your customers happy.

Unfortunately, such basic comprehension is usually missing in the consulting world and, instead, you'll have to make these 20-page powerpoint presentations (all jammed with text in point size 10, of course) to show how complex your projects were and how you've saved yet another day. That's them, the consultants — masters of the universe, saving the world, one powerpoint presentation at a time.

On a more positive note, doing these extracurricular activities does build your public speaking skills, does wonders for your confidence and you learn to easily give presentations at the drop of a hat. Some call it 'going into consulting mode', but whatever you call it, it works and people who take up presentations are always top notch in the public speaking skills department. They almost invariably have clients come up to them after public conferences thanking them for sharing information and ending with attendees grabbing their business card for future reference. So it can't be all bad.

✤ ✤ ✤

Feedback

If there is ever a poster boy for all that a consulting firm wants in an employee, it is someone who is hard-working, affable, ready to lend a hand, a hit with the clients and, most important of all, a team player. He often goes the extra mile to get the job done, but this does not go unnoticed. Or, I should say, he does not let it go unnoticed.

A good consultant is not stupid. He'll learn early on in his career that if you don't toot your own horn, and loudly at that, no one else will. What's worse, with the vultures around you, you had to be quick about it, too, or else they'd be quick to take credit for your work and kick sand in your face.

A good counsellor would have learned that the hard way and would be keen for you to not fall into the same traps. Of course, there were still traps that you'd fall into now and again, but nothing that you couldn't get out of yourself.

Being this superstar, it's not enough to have people think you're great. They need to write it down too and give it to you or your counsellor. This is called 'feedback' in consultant jargon and is one of the most important aspects in managing your career at a consulting firm. Especially feedback that paints you as the best thing to happen since sliced bread.

❄ ❄ ❄

So you would've thought that getting good feedback is just a matter of discussing your objectives with your line manager, achieving them, having a year-end discussion with said manager and then getting the promotion you were promised.

If only it were that easy. There are so many stumbling blocks in getting a promotion, we'll need to dissect this process step by step.

The first problem is in having discussions with your counsellor and setting year-end objectives. If you're lucky, you'll get someone who is not only a good support base, but can also help you from falling into the many traps laid before your path.

Traps colleagues set out for you to fall into on purpose.

More importantly, he will probably be one of the few counsellors that has actually met his counsellees and, what's more, has had regular career discussions with them. I've known colleagues that have met their counsellor just thrice a year — once to discuss goals for the year, another time to discuss mid-year reviews and the third to deliver the inevitable shit sandwich (discussed later in the book), while letting them know that they didn't get the promotion this time. Again.

If that weren't bad enough, just try imagining how tough it is getting written performance reviews. Unlike other jobs, you do not have a fixed set of duties and a permanent manager to report to. In the consulting world, you shift from assignment to assignment until you leave the firm or take an internal transfer. This often means that you, effectively, have a new job every six to eight weeks, along with a new manager to report to and new colleagues to get on your nerves. There are cases where a team stays together on an assignment for say, a year or longer, but these are comparatively rare.

Besides, I'm not so sure whether clients could stand having a full-time army of consultants onsite. Unlike consultants, they actually have to go out into the real world, prove their value to customers and earn some money.

If you're lucky, you'll work for a project manager you like, yet also respect. He's easygoing and fun to be around, yet a tough task master. He won't put up with excuses (particularly if you're hung over from the night before), but he'll lavish praise when you've done a good job.

Unfortunately, this perfect manager is sometimes a mythical creature. More likely, you'll land up with a manager on the job who is himself hung over from last night's drinks, is unfocussed, is unclear what the assignment is all about and probably does not have the skills to run the job. In other words, he was probably more incompetent than all the others on the team put together, but he was in charge and he earned more than any of you.

Someone told me once that he believed in karma and that the universe tends to even things out in the end. When you come across such a situation, it might help to keep this in mind.

Being unfocussed and unintelligent, these types of managers actually turn out to be slippery eels. They know that any words of praise they give in a performance review will be scrutinised thoroughly and so, go to great lengths to avoid giving written feedback altogether. When you go to them at the end of the project and ask them to document all the praise they previously gave you, they'll usually fob you off saying something like, "Don't worry, mate. I know the guys on the review panel and my word will be good enough" or "I'm on the panel myself, so I'll be your biggest cheerleader. Don't worry about a thing."

A person new to the firm would accept them at face value. Don't be that person.

If you have a few years' experience and a promotion under your belt, you'll know how to handle this. Your requests should always in writing and any follow ups are also in writing and include the previous email history and a summary of conversations had. It's so common to do this, it actually has a name — the CYA technique. That stands for 'Cover Your Ass'. That's the only way you can deal with such characters. The other option is to call in your counsellor (who is usually a few ranks senior to you) and they can deliver their bouquets or brickbats to these managers. If you were unfortunate to have a MIA or incommunicado counsellor, well, I guess I can imagine how screwed over you'll feel.

And that is just the problem in getting people to agree to give you feedback. Actually getting it is another hoop to jump through.

❋ ❋ ❋

If you were unlucky to not get the position you interviewed for and took a slightly junior one, you now also have to deal with others who'd been similarly shafted and who wanted to get promoted 'asap', as they like to say in the industry. Great. It was like you're all involved in a bank robbery and the first one to squeal will get the reduced jail sentence while the others languished in prison with life sentences.

If you're fortunate to have a good counsellor, he'll be completely sympathetic to your plight and will do whatever he can to put forward your name for promotion this time around.

A usual stumbling block is that your mid-year reviews will have gone well, but the main feedback was that you need to 'build up your profile'.

This was consultant-speak for taking on more (unpaid) responsibilities. Not just more client-facing work, but things like holding meetings back at the office, giving internal presentations, producing and circulating articles and the like. It's great if you got to take up such responsibilities, but the challenge was in getting people to acknowledge it. In writing.

You'll frequently find that if you'll do all of the above and many managers will come round to your desk saying that your email or presentation was 'so helpful' or 'very interesting', but none of these managers will be willing to give you written feedback that you could use to support your promotion case. At first, you might think it was just a case of plain oversight or that they were being lazy and needed some prodding. Later on, you'll realise that this holding back of feedback was intentional.

Why? Because if I got the feedback and it bolstered my promotion case, where would their counsellees stand? As you may have come to expect, counsellors have targets to meet, too, and not effectively managing your counsellees' careers was not looked upon favourably.

So what better way to kill two birds with one stone by promoting your own counsellee, and then screwing the other guy's protégé? If you were a counsellor, how could you resist?

❀ ❀ ❀

However, that's not the end of the story. You see, at consulting firms, and at most other professional services firms too, the trick to almost getting guaranteed a promotion is excellent client feedback. It's not enough to just do a good job and have your project managers recognise your efforts. It's not enough to stay back after a regular working day and do all those extra-curricular activities like sending out department-wide memos or giving presentations to the wider group.

Oh no, there's one thing, and one thing only, that will virtually guarantee success. And that's great client feedback.

Client feedback at such firms is like Moses coming down from the mountains with the Ten Commandments on two slabs — it is the word of God and cannot be questioned. You'd have to be a fool to do so.

The reasons for this are manifold. Firstly, the client pays your bills. If the guy paying your bills says that you're doing a great job, who are you to question him?

Then, there's the fact that many clients are extremely smart (many are Oxbridge-educated), sometimes even smarter than the consultants sent over to them. So, if the guy who's smarter than you says that you're doing a good job, again, who are you to second-guess him?

Lastly, there's the fact that they actually do something for a living — whether it be flying aircraft, inventing search engines or bringing down the economy, a.k.a being a bank. Consultants, however, just produce reports and spreadsheets and think they're top dog. So, if the guy actually doing something worthwhile in life thinks you're awesome, who is going to question him?

You can now see why client feedback is so treasured and sought after. Get this in hand (along with having ticked off all of the other mundane boxes) and you can pretty much bet on a promotion.

The thing is — and you knew that there had to be a catch somewhere — the clients know this, too. In fact, many of them have crossed over from the consulting field and are old masters of the game. Since they know you would do almost anything for these words from heaven, you end up bending over backwards to keep them happy.

The smart clients will ask for all sorts of reports and extra work, over and above what was agreed to in the contract, and expect all of this for free. Naturally, they will also expect to the wined and dined and they will make sure to always reach for the wine or champagne menus first on such occasions.

The smart consultant will give them their few freebies, but also hold them to account. It is a carrot and stick approach. You scratch my back and I'll scratch yours. So, if your client gets a report that was outside of contract, he had to play ball by writing an nice email to my boss. If you took him out to a fancy dinner and spent £1000s on his bottles of champagne, he needed to send words of praise to your department's managing partner directly.

Most consultants are reticent in doing this as they are not sure whether they can make such demands from their clients. However, it is just a matter of asking them tactfully and politely and, in most cases, your wish will be granted. Some colleagues will have no tact at all and will ask for feedback for the smallest of things. The trick was to delight clients, surprise them, make them feel like they're so unique in the industry (when, matter-of-factly, it was only the logo that changes), and they will do pretty much whatever you wanted. Charm and persuasion will carry you much further than you'd imagine.

It's important to know which side of the bread was buttered and to pull out all the stops to get these scant lines of praise. A client that does not play ball is usually dealt with by finishing the job as quickly as possible and getting out of there. There is no need to spend any more time on a client that is not going to be valuable to you.

❀ ❀ ❀

The Shit Sandwich

Have you heard of the 'shit sandwich'?
Doesn't sound very appetising, does it?
Well, it isn't meant to be. Besides, it's not
a meal. It's a style of performance review.

The basic theory is that employees these
days cannot handle constructive criticism.
Instead, you have to soften your language
and surround your message with positive
praise. You start off with saying
something positive that the staff member
has done, follow it up with the actual
feedback you wish to convey and then
wrap things up with another meaningless
bunch of tripe so that they feel good about
themselves.

Yep, a shit sandwich.

Allow me to illustrate via feedback that was once given to me:

Layer of bread: "Your clients love you. You handle things aplomb, projects are never late and the deliverables are top notch."

Layer of shit: "You are never in the office and the partners are worried about your visibility. Given that you want to progress to senior manager next year, it might be a good idea to raise your visibility with some department-wide activities."

Layer of bread: "You've got really good feedback from your subordinates and you've clearly managed challenging situations with tricky staff members. You'll go a long way. You're on the right trajectory."

In other words, they're happy that I'm managing client projects and staff members (which, as I recall, was in my job spec), but in spite of being a client-based job, they want me to spend more time in the office doing useless things like organising team meetings, away days, strategy sessions and corporate social responsibility activities.

Put simply, they want to squeeze blood from stone and own your soul.

So you now have employees being in the position of having to give and receive these shit sandwiches. It's a non-stop process right throughout the year. Any let up and you lose the chance of getting positive feedback from line managers at mid-year and year-end review sessions. Suddenly, they 'forget' about you and all the hard work you've done. Particularly on their projects. Funny that.

So, you need to catch them while the project is coming to a close and get their feedback in writing. Any promise of theirs to speak up on your behalf at the year-end deliberations is probably a lie and a way of getting out of putting anything in writing.

Meanwhile, as a manager, you're stuck with a bunch of idiots for staff members who all want positive feedback in spite of their work being crap and you having to re-do it or asking them to re-do it. So, you have to adopt the shit sandwich approach when giving them feedback, too.

The trick here, then, is to make the layer of crap in the feedback process to sound so innocuous that it really doesn't hold you back for the promotion process.

Things like 'raising visibility', etc. can be easily rectified by sending a few emails here and there and hosting the occasional team meeting or drinks events. Be wary of committing to too much as you've got to have a life too. However, if you serious about a promotion and want to pull out all the stops, go all in. Emails summarising technical briefs, links to industry articles, hosting internal meetings, organising team or, better yet, departmental meetings, leading client pitches — the list is virtually limitless.

❊ ❊ ❊

Performance Reviews

This is the most important section of this part of the book. Performance reviews can make or break your career at a consulting firm, so focus on this and most other things will fall into place.

Performance review season usually takes place twice a year — one a mid-year assessment and the other the end-of-year assessment. We need to have a mid-year review to see if you're 'on track to achieve your year-end goals' and then a year-end review to assess whether 'you've met the goals you set out'. I don't know about you, but it should seem like a five-minute affair each, even if you have to do the blasted thing twice a year.

A performance review means that all the work you've done in the past couple of months has to count for something. A good performance review could result in either a solid pay increase or a promotion (which also had a built-in pay rise, though not as much as you'd think). Cue intense listening to 'The Final Countdown' by 1980s pop band Europe when preparing your review papers. Nothing like some cheesy '80s pop to get your spirits up.

However, it's not all smooth sailing. Let me explain how a performance review takes place at a consulting (or any other professional services) firm.

Firstly, it is not something that managers do when they feel that they've identified talent and want to promote that individual. Oh, no. You see, these organisations are multinational, global ones so they've got devoted HR teams to do that. That means you have a whole department filled with individuals who are under-qualified to get a job in real life and who pretend to be intelligent by speaking in gender-neutral terms and all communicate in one dull, monotonous, androgynous tone.

So you now have this team full of HR 'professionals', 'business partners' or whatever their job title of the day is, who know nothing about the business or its complexities, but now seem to have magically presented themselves to management as experts, telling them how to do their job, how to spot talent and how to groom the leaders of tomorrow. You can't make this up. Even the best management consultant would have to hand it to them.

Unfortunately, given the lopsided politically-correct nature of the modern workplace, I hardly suspect that any one consulting firm (or other major global firms) is in this unique position. In organisation after organisation I've visited in my professional career, I've seen the same thing over and over again. Smart, yet hapless, managers unable to get their work done due to clueless HR mangers barking out orders based on some pre-ordained, opaque notion of how managers are to do their jobs. Hence, the rise of trial lawyers and a generation of a society where any criticism of an employee's performance is considered 'bullying'.

But that's not the end of it. You'll have to prepare reams of paper, fill in forms on multiple systems and generally waste a lot of dead trees printing these sets out. In triplicate, like in some third-world country's bureaucracy. Then, you'll have to suffer the ignominy of having your efforts rubbished by a 'review panel' constituted of many other bozos in the department, many of whom you have never actually worked with. Suddenly these guys are in a position to comment on your work and give you career advice? Alas, such is life in a consulting firm.

❊ ❊ ❊

When you think of a consulting gig at a major professional services firm, the image built up is one of working in plush offices, working with talented colleagues and with smart and engaging clients in exotic destinations like London, New York, Paris, Tokyo, Sydney, Singapore or Hong Kong.

What if, instead, you worked 80-100 hours a week, at some vague site in Hull, with colleagues that have a personality more vapid than an empty soft drink can and with clients who either don't know what they're doing or don't care?

Welcome to life in consulting at a top-tier professional services firm.

Couple this with the fact that you don't really earn top-tier money until you hit senior manager or above and you can see the scene for what it really is — a scam. The workplace operates in the form of a pyramid scheme where there are fewer and fewer positions available as you move up the ranks. Competition gets more intense and, before long, the daggers come out.

Bear in mind that as the years go by, there's even greater competition and, to get the upper hand, candidates will usually resort to dirty tricks' campaigns and outright slandering each other when the other person is not around. It's brutal and vicious, but before you think that the bosses will put a stop to it, think again. They thrive on the covertly hostile environment as they know that, like leaving crabs in an open box, you will pull each other down as you don't want to see the next guy succeed. It is so blatant that some people even stop smiling to each other or wishing each other when they meet. They will have been tightly wound up by their counsellors, no doubt, and any sign of weakness, even something as benign as a smile or making polite conversation, is ruled out as being for wimps.

It may almost getting to the point of open warfare sometimes and you'd be best advised not taking any chances. Go in with all guns blazing to get this promotion and don't take no for an answer.

❊ ❊ ❊

More importantly, you must have clear in your mind what you want to come out of the performance review. You could make up your mind to at least get a pay raise, if nothing else. Failing that, some tough it out for a few more months, possibly a year, before leaving the funny farm for other pastures.

What happens if you don't get it? Well, you could do what everyone else who's been rejected does — stick it to these guys and get another job.

It is a brutal world and seeing once erstwhile colleagues now becoming your bosses can be hard for the ego to handle. As with many other things in life, it helps to know thyself, especially one's failings.

In these sorts of firms, image plays a very important role, probably more important than performance and intelligence itself. It's like that in many things in life, but in consulting firms, it was probably the main thing that decided whether you stayed or moved on, whether you were promoted or not and, most important of all, whether you got a good pay raise or not. So, even if you couldn't give a toss about these things, it made sense to play the game and not jump out of the box too much or, more accurately, when you know it's safe to do so.

❄ ❄ ❄

Review Panels

Review panels are where managers more senior to you and the partners get together to discuss your performance. They do this in batches so that no one candidate comes out on top and the others pushed all the way to the bottom. It's mean, in theory, to be a 'moderating process' so that candidates are assessed on their own performance as well as in comparison to that of their peers.

If your counsellor is smart, he will have gone into the review panels fully prepared, but not before finding out who he'd be presenting your case to. There may be the off chance that he has worked with these panel members in the past and, thus, could use his own past performance to boost your chances at the presentation. A chip of the old block, as it were.

Coming out of the review panels, the conversation with your counsellor could go one of two ways. If you get promoted to manager, great. Pop out the champagne bottles!

If not, you'll get some predictable line like: "What do you have to worry about? After all, you're young. If you miss this year's promotion rounds, there's always next year. At the year-end review, everyone mentioned how much potential you have to be a future leader in the firm."

Sometimes, no concrete reason will be given, but you will receive the usual trope of 'future potential', 'going a long way in the firm', 'solid performer', etc.

I won't kid you. It can be very disheartening to learn that you did not get the promotion you worked so hard for.

Even more so when it is given to someone else who, for example, was on secondment at a client's office for the best part of the year and no one on the team really knowing what she looks like. True life incident, by the way.

Sometimes, the universe is just not fair and it helps to be a believer at these times.

❉ ❉ ❉

If you're wondering why grown men and women in the consulting industry perform like circus monkeys, jumping through all these hoops, running around for pieces of feedback to bolster their year-end reviews, etc, it is because the sad truth is that they are vastly underpaid for the work they do.

I wish to be clear. There are other people in society that do much more important things, but get paid a fraction of what they earn — nurses, teachers and firefighters immediately come to mind.

But, the consulting world, much like the banking industry, lives in its own bubble. It can't see much beyond the narrow confines of its offices or that of its clients.

As an employee, a consultant's focus is to only look for the next pay rise and the next promotion. Anything beyond that is not worth thinking about.

Besides, you'll be surprised to hear that a lot of people that work in financial services and its related industries (law, accountancy, consulting and the like) are pretty much knee-deep in debt. It's not like they are living on the poverty line or anything, but there are certainly quite a few that depend on the money and the lavish lifestyle it provides, while others depend on the credit card to keep them afloat until pay day.

That's the biggest trap to fall into — lifestyle inflation. As your pay increases, you spend more money and therefore need more at the end of the month to balance your books. The monthly outgo just gets higher and higher as the years go by and before you know it, you need that promotion or pay rise just to maintain your lifestyle.

Memories of toughening it out on a meagre student budget, yet having some of the best days of your lives are soon forgotten and you fall victim to purchasing the latest consumer electronic device or going on vacation to the latest travel destination of the year.

In many ways, they are the 1% of society (or, more accurately, among the 5%). They are among the top taxpayers in the country and have life better than a vast majority of the working population. But when you live in a bubble, your friends live in this same bubble and you all think alike, objectivity and gratitude become your enemies and prevent you from taking a balanced view of life.

The partners in the firm know this and so dangle the carrot of either a promotion or a pay rise to keep you working ever longer hours. It's easy to get angry at them, but, hey, no one forced you to work here!

At the end of the day, though, when you come back into the bubble on the morning train and you work with clients who are bankers or hedge fund mangers wearing bespoke suits and luxury Swiss watches, you feel underpaid. And, therefore, inadequate. Hence, the need to constantly be running this treadmill to obtain that pay rise or promotion.

The smart ones stick long enough to get a good block of experience on their CV and then negotiate their way to a better-paying job. The losers settle into a career at the consulting firm as they know that they would not cut it in the real world and instead reconcile themselves to being a circus monkey performing these degrading tricks for the rest of their working lives.

As I mentioned before, know thyself and choose wisely.

At this point, it's probably helpful to take a moment to reflect. Of course, in all your shared moments with friends at work, you'll always talk of quitting and going somewhere else. Everyone does it. It is par for the course. It's just that not many pull the trigger and actually do it.

In fact, here you might find yourself going in the opposite direction — going deeper into the abyss and gunning for a higher position and bigger pay-stub. If anything, you will see erstwhile colleagues cashing out of the casino just when the going is good, while you seem to be doubling down on your bets and going all in.

❊ ❊ ❊

If you're going for a senior manager's role, there's a slight change in the pecking order. You'll still need the stellar client and colleague feedback and you'll still need to have a thoroughly briefed (and engaged) counsellor, but you'll need to make a presentation yourself to the review panels. This is the big show and you're the main attraction. Don't screw this up.

As for the presentation itself, you have ten minutes to make your presentation (which will go faster than you think), followed by around 15 minutes of questioning by the panel. You'll be peppered with questions as to what you achieved on projects, why you deserve to be promoted to senior manager and what growth opportunities you can bring to the firm if they promote you. You then leave the room while the panel members have another five minutes to deliberate and collectively gather their thoughts. All in all, each candidate has about 30 minutes in total and, to be fair, the panel members do not entertain overruns and extensions. After all, if the presentation for your own promotion overran, how could you be expected to manage projects and staff members without overruns.

Whatever the case, be confident. If you've made it this far, there's only the last mile left and you can do this. When it comes to your presentation, practise, practise and practise again. However, get a good night's sleep the night before and wake up refreshed, rather than ending up a bundle of nerves with last-minute presentations and changes to your pitch.

It's imperative to get your 60-second elevator-pitch down to the tee. Once that's done, go full swing into the actual business case and then wrap it up with some client feedback. If you've done your homework, you'll hit this one out of the park.

❀ ❀ ❀

If you do get the promotion, well, congratulations!

I know it's a big achievement getting to senior manager and all that, but quite frankly, the feeling won't be as sweet as you think it'll be. The last few months would have been gruelling, so it'll take some time for the elation to sink in. In the beginning, though, you'll just feel relief and long for some much-required sleep.

A month ago, you were at manager level and therefore only had limited experience to be of value to anyone. Now, you're a senior manager and you're dishing out advice as if you're some sort of sage at the top of a mountain. Everyone, clients included, lap it up without batting an eyelid. If you told them that their competitors had now mandated that their employees come to work in pink shirts and lime-green trousers, I am sure more than a few would actively consider it.

I don't know whether such power is something to be proud of, or fearful of. I'll leave it to you to decide.

Soon, the euphoria will wear off, though, and you'll gain in confidence as you realise that you're now running huge projects for Fortune 500 or FTSE 100 companies all by yourself. Just be sure to keep your feet on the ground, stay close to your roots and not let things get to your head. I've seen many a character start acting like absolute idiots once they get promoted to senior manager and they walk around thinking they're the biggest thing to hit town since sliced bread. Before you know it, no one wants to work with them, partners included, and these guys are at sea without a life vest or lifebuoy.

It's not an easy ride, being here in a consulting firm. They find newer ways to squeeze blood from stone every year and your targets will just seem to get higher and higher, staff morale and energy levels be damned. It's a miracle no one has thrown a lawsuit in their direction alleging unfair labour practices. If this were a factory, they'd have been shut down a long time ago.

Now that you're one of the senior members of staff, it means people will now look up to you for inspiration and any small mistake on your part will be analysed to bits.

It also means that you'll be left largely on your own. You'll need to pick up your own assignments, pick your bosses to work for and, most important of all, pick your own battles. I know that you may have had to be combative at times to get to senior manager, but with your new role comes a lot of expectation and responsibility. Your saving grace will be the excellent work that you put in and the fact that your clients love you. But, sometimes, you'll feel that even that isn't enough.

Once you get to senior manager, you need to be doubly careful. I'm not saying that you need to be a kiss-ass or anything like that, but you may need to beef up your diplomacy skills, now that you'll pretty much be on your own. They say it gets lonely at the top and that's definitely the case when you're one of the chosen few to have won a gruelling and hard-fought battle to get to senior manager.

At this stage, you're in the big leagues now. If you don't hone these much-required skills, and fast, you won't last very long. Such offices are ruthless and you need to have eyes at the back of your head, just so that you could see the ones coming up to stab you in the back. The environment here is vicious. It is a dog-eat-dog world and the faster you adapted to it, the better your chances of survival. However, you still need the grace and diplomacy to smile while stabbing your enemies.

❊ ❊ ❊

Don't Trip Up

Leading up to performance review time, you'll sometimes be put on a project with someone of the same rank of you.

Normally, it's not a problem, but since you're both going in for promotion, you have to make sure you come out on top. More than that, you can bet that the other guy is going to put his foot out for you to trip over. The primary task, then, is to make sure that you don't trip and, if possible (and if you want to), to pull a switcheroo and make sure he trips up.

Normally, in cases where there were only junior staff, you'd take the lead and be reporting directly to the partner. But in this case, since your 'nemesis' and you are of equal rank and stature, the partner will not want to rock the boat and so will not appoint anyone in charge. Officially, that is.

If the partner is not on your side, you can bet that he and your nemesis will be concocting schemes for him to come out on top yet leaving you holding the bag, if ever anything were to go awry.

Their plan, in such instances, will be for the other to 'take charge' of the assignment and to relegate you to a supporting actor's role. If the partner wants his charge to get the promotion this year, he will pull out all the stops for his golden boy to get it.

Normally, I'd suggest ignoring such office politics as it was just one assignment where you'd have to take the back seat. If someone else wanted to feel like the big kahuna, did it really matter? After all, everyone gets their fifteen minutes of fame.

But you're going for promotion this year, too, and so need to be seen to be in charge of staff members (including peers) in order to make it to the next grade, particularly if you're going for senior manager.

Whenever you have a meeting with the partner, and your nemesis starts to say something, wait for the inevitable stumble and then cut in with, "Well, actually Mr. Partner, the client said such and such and I proposed a solution to their problem, which they received quite well. But Nemesis here is coping quite well, all things considered."

Make the other guy look like a fool (which, naturally, he is) at every given opportunity. Otherwise, he'll do the same to you.

Other tricks to watch out for include: scheduling client meetings without you being invited, being given last-minute deadlines to meet, handling inane queries from junior colleagues thereby distracting you and wasting your time, etc.

❊ ❊ ❊

Lobbying Groups

Okay, so you didn't get the promotion the first time around. That's, dare I say it, normal. So don't beat yourself up about it too much.

You then decide to go for it the next time around.

However, now the competition has become more brutal than before and favouritism is so rife and open that sometimes you feel that there is just no point in even trying. Still, I admire the ones that deserved it, worked hard for it, knew that they were not going to get it, but still put in their business case just so that they could get that slap in the face from management.

On the face of it, you might think that going into a process that you were guaranteed to lose was a suicide mission and a total waste of time. In any other industry, I'd be totally inclined to agree with you.

However, this is the consulting industry and in organisations such as these, the normal rules of sanity don't apply and you have to make things happen in order to make things happen.

If that sounds confusing, allow me to explain. Like real life, consulting is also filled with lobbyists, albeit of a different kind.

❁ ❁ ❁

Sometimes, you'll see colleagues being seemingly rapidly rushed through the ranks, in spite of their lack of experience or, worse, their very clear lack of intelligence.

That's because they're probably an active member of one of the consulting firm's various 'support networks' which, among other things, is a firm-sponsored internal lobbying group to get women, minorities or whoever to advance within the firm.

While seemingly innocuous, you'll soon learn that the group's members and its aims are quite sinister. Their unstated, but clear-as-daylight, aim is usually to advance their members within the firm, even if they were not qualified for the job.

For some reason, members felt that being in one of these cherished groups qualified you for a promotion, hard work and results be damned. There will be bi-weekly meetings after work where strategies will be discussed on how to get promotions, increase visibility, etc. All and sundry ideas were discussed, except actually working hard and bringing home the bacon.

Worse still, many of its senior members were on promotion panels and will blatantly push for the advancement of these groups' members in spite of other, more qualified candidates being better deserving. Alas, this being the modern-day consulting firm, the promotion process will often got swept up in the madness of political correctness and the ranks are littered with clearly incompetent people who had no reason for being so high up.

In summary, try and get on one of these groups, as it will look good in your review panel papers. The lobbying mafia may just give you that extra push you need to get that promotion.

❊ ❊ ❊

Secondments

A secondment is when your firm loans a staff member to your client. The employee is still on the consulting firm's books and pays their salary, but said staff member is directly under the control of the client. He is expected to work to their times and meet their job spec.

Consulting firms have a love-hate relationship with secondments.

The firm hates secondments because it means loaning your staff members away for relatively long periods. Time that could have been spent earning the firm more money, as secondment assignments are very poor earners. They are usually done to maintain good client relationships. The firm gets practically nothing out of it and it is, in some ways, just a PR or marketing exercise. Plus, if the client actually likes the employee, they may make them a job offer (even though they're not allowed to, by contract). For a consultant, it's very difficult to say no to a client who is really chuffed with your work, whom you interact with on a daily basis and get along with and is willing to double your salary overnight.

It's very difficult for an employee to say no and consulting firms hate it for this very reason, as do other professional services firm such as accountants, lawyers and the like. The firm would rather lose an employee to a competitor as it knows that their pay bands are largely in line and therefore wages in the industry can be artificially kept low. Competing with clients of yours for talented staff, especially when they have deeper pockets, is not a game you could ever hope to win. So the firm makes it up to secondees in other ways with promises of a promotion or a hefty pay rise.

Before you get all teary-eyed for your local neighbourhood consulting firm, the situation works in their favour too.

Internally, among staff members, secondments are viewed as a banishment. In many cases, where the consulting firm has no need for a particular employee, they have been sent out on secondment, in the hope that the client will like them and therefore offer them a job. It's a win-win for everybody. The firm gets rid of someone it doesn't need or want without causing a scene, the client gets to try before it buys and the employee in question…well he (or she) probably had no future here, so he'd take whatever he could get, especially if it came with a pay increase. Everybody's happy. Hurrrah!

❀ ❀ ❀

Wining and Dining

In this line, the normal thing to do is to wine and dine the client, quite literally, at the end of the project. That way you've recovered the money from the client and have something to spend on dinner and wine.

However, your marketing department may tip you off that the client is having problems with its main consulting services provider, which just happens to be your competitor. You're keen to steal the account and so will have to pull out all the stops to win them over.

❊ ❊ ❊

I'd recommend making reservations for dinner at one of the top restaurants in the

City. The bill is going to run into the thousands but, quite frankly, who cares?

Your management will usually authorise this extravagance since they've got some money in the marketing budget they've appropriated to blow up on the affair. They're determined to win the account at all costs and will help you pull out all the stops to make sure everything is running tickety-boo.

It's a good thing that client's staff members are usually all 40-plus. These folks are low maintenance. For them, dinner and wine is a good night out. But that doesn't mean it was going to come cheap. There was a virtual open bar and clients use it as an opportunity to buy aged wines, exquisite champagnes bottles and all the spirit they can hold. Food is ordered aplenty and, sadly, equally wasted too. It's as if they've never seen food before and they end up ordering just about everything on the menu just because they can.

If you were to travel less than three miles east of the City, you'd come across people begging on the streets for food and joints selling you a kebab for less than a fiver. The contrast couldn't be more stark, but most will never see it. Such is life in the bubble.

❊ ❊ ❊

Once you're done with pleasantries over starters, try and entertain the client with an amusing tale of how a rival of theirs (no names, of course) got into trouble with their regulator. Half way through the story, you should pause for dramatic effect.

Don't let the pause continue longer than necessary and quickly resume the story, much to the client's delight. Leave the story on a high as to how you or your firm helped save the day. While seemingly banal, the client will remember this in his hungover condition tomorrow morning and remember to call you the next time his regulator comes knocking on his door.

✱ ✱ ✱

Let's be clear, however. Your clients are not really interested in your work. They just want the report card to say that they have an 'A' and then they can show that to their boss or regulator and get a sweet reward (i.e. a hefty annual bonus). They don't really care about the quality of work you put in or your long hours.

To be frank, why should they? They're only looking for the annual bonus that pays for their new family sedan every second year, the annual vacation in the sun and the ever-increasing shambles that has become the university funding system.

So, by all means, get close to them and become their confidant of sorts, but keep in mind that this is a working relationship only.

In many ways, these types of clients are the best as they know that they don't know all the answers, but want to get the experts in and help them out. I have less interest in the other types that think they know better than us and are in this constant one-upmanship battle to prove it. They usually end up losing, but it results in a lot of bruised egos, a switch to our competitors, then back to us when they realise that our competitors are probably worse. But this time, they return with more emotional baggage and a score to settle.

❀ ❀ ❀

When you get recruited for any project, it's always a challenge to know whom you're actually serving and whose interests to keep in mind. For example, the pitch you're working on could say that the head of finance has called in for tenders. That's all fine and dandy, but who is actually going to use your report? Is it the managing director, who wants to tell his regulatory agency that everything is hunky-dory? Is it the finance director that actually wants to get rid of the head of finance and so wants to use your report as a pretext to fire him? Is it the project sponsor who wants to use this report as a weapon to make changes elsewhere in the firm? You can never tell.

Get this right and you're on your way to collecting handsome fees. Get it wrong and you can get all sorts of complaints on how things are not working out, how the project is running beyond budget, etc.

✣ ✣ ✣

Looking for a Change

The phone rings just as you're doing your last expense envelope for the week. It's an unlisted number. You'd normally ignore those, but it could be a client, so you pick up.

"Hi, Consultant. This is Ollie Whitfield from the Line Norton recruitment agency. How are you mate?"

You don't know this guy. What does he want from you?

"Um…I'm fine, Ollie, thanks. Have we met before?" you reply.

"Not in person, but I caught your details on the internet and thought that I'd give you a ring to find out where you are in your career and if you're looking for a change?"

Oh, God. Not the old "looking for a change" routine. This guy is fishing for leads and is just wasting your time.

In such situations, it pays to make your apologies and tell him that you aren't looking for a new job, nor did you know anyone else who was, but that you'd keep in touch if something should change.

Beware though. They now have your number and will pester you every couple of months to find out if you've changed my mind.

Bloody recruitment agents. You invariably needed their assistance when looking to move on, but they would hound you even after getting you a new job. It was not unknown for a recruiter to call you six months into the new job you're in and ask you if you're looking for a change. Six months! Just enough to get past your probation period and their no-poach clause to expire.

Keep your distance from these guys when you have a job, but be sure to keep their contact details handy for when you are going to be 'looking for a change'.

❉ ❉ ❉

Name Change

There's something about consulting firms and their constant changing of internal business unit names, business titles and reporting lines. It's not unknown for one to join a consulting firm and undergo several rebranding exercises before leaving.

These reorganisations happen about every 18 to 24 months. It's like some partner higher up the ladder gets antsy and decides to moves teams around and rename them just to keep things fresh. In the three or so years most people stay in consulting before moving on, they will have already been through two reorganisations and I'm sure one more is on its way, just around the corner, as they walk out the revolving doors on their last day at work.

* * *

Murphy's Law

One of the major rules in life in consulting is that things never go according to plan. This line of work epitomised Murphy's law and it is a miracle that consultants were still in business. Come to think of it, this happened with all the other consultants out there (including those at professional services firms), so it's more likely that clients didn't have a choice and had to put up with budget overruns, missed deadlines and less-than-stellar consultants showing up.

If you're the conscientious type of worker, you'll get freaked about such things happening all around you. But there's no need to panic. Just focus on your projects and keep them humming along. Ignore the office gossip about someone else's project going tits up and how they are looking for a scapegoat. Keep your head down and soldier on.

* * *

Away Days and Corporate Jollies

Ah, away days. The company takes you to some exotic location to reveal their new 'go-to market strategy' or some new 'product/solution' to flog onto your unsuspecting clients. If nothing else, there will be a lot of affairs going on and marriages breaking up or new relationships formed as a result of this corporate jolly.

These events come very rarely, so make the most of them.

If you're male, you're in luck. This place/event will be heaving with action. Seriously. The crowd will be something like 60% female and 99% of them will be totally fit.

At first, you'll think that this was like giving matches to a kid surrounded by gunpowder. I don't know whose idea it is to send young people off on an all-expense-paid trip to some exotic location and then expect them to work, but who the cares? It's one of the perks of the job and no one will say no to it.

❄ ❄ ❄

Conferences like these happen only once in a while, so it's up to you to make the most of it. Some people use it to actually learn stuff; some use it to progress their careers; most others use it as an excuse to party away from their spouses.

If it's three things you can guarantee at such conferences, it would be the following: there's always going to be the over-eager types who want to shine and use it in their promotion cases (you know, they showed 'leadership' when all they did was ramble on through some thoroughly boring Powerpoint presentation); another set would use it as an opportunity to get totally lagered up as wine and beer flow freely at such events and an open bar is always a temptation too strong to resist; the last category could be defined in only one word: sex.

These jollies were a known orgy. Think about it: you're here away from you fat/ugly/repugnant/nagging/balding/flaccid/cellulite-heavy spouse; most probably in some beautiful (and warm) location; away from your nosy, prying neighbours; away from the brats that your sweet, loving children have become; and, all your expenses are taken care of. What's not to love?

Add bikinis and alcohol to the mix and you can pretty much be sure that someone is going to get pregnant during the course of the jaunt; someone else is going to get divorced six months later; and, many a couple will form their relationship here in the throes of passion, baked by the intense heat of the location.

In other words, this is HR's worst nightmare come true.

❀ ❀ ❀

If you're in a larger conference, there's more fun to be had. Some people, no names of course, have used this as an opportunity to do a bit of company-sponsored sightseeing instead of attending the whole conference. I pass no moral judgement on this and any action you take in this regard is entirely your responsibility.

With that out of the way, let's see how some people have used this to their advantage. (Note: this probably only works at conferences where the attendance is in the hundreds or even thousands, as your absence will be noticed at smaller ones.)

You usually sign into a delegates' register and you get a pass that slings around our neck. Not only are you supposed to carry and display it at all times, but the barcodes on it will also be used to scan your entry into the various sessions over

the course of the conference and record
your attendance.

As you sign up, you'll doubt whether even
prisons had such an elaborate attendance
registration system. Moreover, the need to
carry it dangling from your necks will
make you look like wild animals in a zoo,
being led around your caged enclosures
by your masters, looking for scraps of
food to be thrown your way at lunchtime
and, if you behaved well, you were let out
into the hotel gardens or pools to play for
a while. If it's one thing that such firms are
good at, it is in making you feel like their
pet poodle. They feel that just because
they paid you a salary, they owned you
and that you are to do all that they want,
no matter your personal circumstances,
your need for a personal life or the fact
that you had other interests outside of

work. This place demands absolute devotion and they will get it, one way or another.

If you manage to put aside your seething resentment at the need for these 'dog collars', just go with the flow for now.

The security at such events is not all that great. It's just so easy to skip sessions, yet still record full attendance.

At multi-day conferences, they use the barcode scanners to register your attendance only in the mornings, for the first session, and again at the first session after lunch. The rest of the day, you're pretty much free to do whatever you want.

What a stroke of genius this is. Obviously, the person who thought it up must be pretty daft if he expects a bunch of 20- and 30-somethings to attend boring conferences the whole day. But for those of you looking to have a good time in whatever exotic locale you're in — which, quite frankly speaking, is just about anyone — this is a spot of good luck. You only had to sign in twice a day and the rest was up to you.

Of course, you'd still need to make the occasional appearance to keep up image. Even better, if you were really smart, you'd pop into a session or two and ask some really tough question at the Q&A session at the end. This way, you'd be remembered as the guy who had interesting questions and could always use it to defend yourself when questioned about your absence. Such tricks will come second nature to you when you are in the consulting business.

What could be better than knowing that you could game the system so that you had a guaranteed vacation at company expense?

❊ ❊ ❊

Consulting Lingo

If there's one thing you learn very quickly in your first year of management consulting, it's that your current vocabulary is rubbish. You don't have any worthwhile verbal skills to speak of.

Oh sure, maybe you aced your English language exams in school or university or even majored in languages at an Oxbridge institution. But when you join a consulting firm, you have to effectively start from square one again.

You see, language here is all important. It's the only way you can justify clients paying you the big bucks that they do, for what even a high-school teenager could have told you if you explained the situation to him in simple terms. It's often been said that the definition of a consultant is one that borrows your watch to tell you the time. That has never been more true than dealing with clients that are banks, insurance companies, hedge funds, pension managers and the like.

If it's one skill the management consultant needs, it's the ability to talk his way through tricky situations, while still getting the client to pay for this garbage advice. Not only do you borrow the client's watch to tell him the time, but you also charge him for the privilege.

Any sane person would know that when things are going wrong, you take a breather, analyse the situation, possibly compare with your peers, arrive at a solution and implement it. Rinse and repeat. It's not rocket science and that's just the way it should be.

Unfortunately, modern-day corporate life is a little bit more complicated than that.

You have clients that are perennially insecure about their standing, not just in their organisation, but also among their peers. It's a constant game of one-upmanship and consultants are welcome players in this silly game.

You could be making the pitch of your life to a prospective client and be on the verge of losing it, but just throw in a few juicy nuggets about how you know what their peers are doing, what direction the industry is headed in (even though consultants sometimes barely have a clue as to what their clients actually do) or

what their regulator is up to and, before
you know it, your clients are sitting up in
their seats, all perked up and attentive.
You now have them in your hands and
they are powerless. They can't help
themselves. They must know what their
peers are up to and what their regulator
has in store for them, so they now cross
the Rubicon from passive indifference to
actually making your case to their
superiors as to why you should be hired
on the spot and brought in right away to
help them set things right.

A successful consultant knew what
buttons to press and when.

In the computer industry (as it was
known back then), someone once said
long ago, "No one gets fired for buying
IBM." It's another matter that IBM is

hardly what we consider an innovator these days (as we stare longingly at the slabs of glass that our smartphones have become), but the logic still held true back in the day. You could take a chance by going for a smaller or lesser-known computer supplier, but if things went tits up (and they invariably did), you'll be on the hook as to why you hired Joe Bloggs Limited instead of going for IBM. Sure, you might have saved a ton of bob on the contract, but now things had gone wrong and you had to pay with your scalp.

If, however, you had not strayed from the pack and instead went with IBM, even if the project screwed up or your machines went kaput, you could always turn around to your superiors, shrug your shoulders and say, "But I hired IBM and they're the biggest in the business. If they got

something wrong, this must truly be a monumental problem. So, don't blame me."

Job done. IBM still got its money, you still had your job and your managers would up the budget to 'rectify' the problem or pay for a 'solution', whatever that happened to be. No one cares that the buffoons at IBM shouldn't have screwed up in the first place (being the 'experts' that they are) or that you should have negotiated a better contract to protect against such screwups. All that is inconsequential. You hired the best in the business and if even they couldn't get a grip on the problem, it must truly be complex.

No one gets fired for buying IBM.

In much the same way, going for a big brand-name consulting, accounting or legal firm is pretty much the same scenario. There are bright and capable individuals in smaller and equally global firms, but these firms don't have the brand recognition that the big ones do. In effect, a client is buying an insurance policy for himself. If things go wrong, he can always say that he hired this big-name consultancy, which he considered the best, and if even the bright boys and girls there can't get it right, the problem must be a really tough nut to crack.

Before you laugh at the absurdity of the situation, think about its consequences. For one thing, you have a concentration of power in a handful of firms that all think and behave alike. There is, quite possibly, no difference, apart from corporate logo,

from the work any given consulting firm and its peers produce. It's the same, bland, jargon-filled reports that get commissioned, get reviewed for all of five minutes and then flung into the corner, never to be seen or read again.

So what, you may say. Fair point. But you just have to see the office reception of one of these prestigious firms and notice that all their employees are alike — same corporate garb, same haircuts, same style of speaking and, most disturbingly, a massive overdose of groupthink and a genuine lack of insight (no matter what the brochures or pitches say).

Secondly, let's not forget that consultants don't come cheap. They charge premium rates and the consumer is the real loser in this equation as they now have to pay for

a higher cost of goods and services. That cement you bought for your loft extension? Maybe it would have been 5-10% cheaper had its management decided to not hire consultants and instead pull their heads out of their backsides and notice that quality standards were slipping to the detriment of customer satisfaction.

Or how about the prized jewel in the UK — the beloved National Health Service? Instead of hiring an army of useless paper-filling middle managers and an equally large battalion of consultants, how about just letting doctors and nurses (you know, the ones who actually know what they're doing) get on with their jobs and then reduce the cost of our healthcare, even if it's a few hundred million quid a year.

Better yet, how about getting rid of the army of consultants, law firms, lobbyists and the sort from Parliament and asking our representatives and civil servants to actually do some work and get results. Instead, we have politicians and bureaucrats just passing the buck and saying that they relied on the experts for input.

But then, we would have world peace and where would that leave us? No, instead, let's continue the system of having big brand-name consultants flood our offices and protect us from getting fired. Everyone is happier that way. More pertinently, everyone wants it to remain that way.

No one gets fired for buying IBM.

So you now have an environment where consultants are not only 'required' but also have the red carpet rolled out for them. Best not to disappoint, then, and to keep to the image that clients expect of you.

❊ ❊ ❊

If I held a pen in my hand and asked you to name it, what would you say? I'm going to go out on a limb and guess you're going to say, "a pen".

Correct. But, in the consulting world, we would not describe it as a pen. It would be called a 'thought transcribing apparatus' or a 'idea generator'.

What about a cup of water?

I would rather describe it as a 'liquid refreshment enabler' or a 'thirst-quenching receptacle'. I hope you get my point now.

What if I pointed to my laptop? Would you be tempted to describe it as an 'information communication device'?

That would be a good start. A better description would be a 'knowledge transformation equipment capable of gigawatt processing and full-throttle information metamorphosis'. Gives it a bit more oomph, don't you think?

Coming back to real life, you can always tell the client that you'll review his documents and provide feedback. That's great, but it sounds so plain. Instead, say you will 'perform a top-to-bottom analysis' of his data, run 'concerted benchmarking against best practices' and finally 'document key facts and findings in a tabular format that highlights the key vulnerabilities that are summarised in a SWOT analysis'. All before he's even had the chance to digest lunch.

Best way to find out if you've put in a lot of tosh is to see if a fellow consultant can understand it. If he can, job done. If, however, the partner's secretary can understand it, it's back to the drawing board as it's probably too pedestrian.

Ultimately, when you finalise the pitch or deliverables, be sure to put the higher ups on cc. You might be tempted to effectively run solo and handle all client communications from your inbox, especially if you're senior manager. It gives you a sense of power and massively boots your ego. But who are you going to blame when things go awry?

Remember: Murphy's Law is always lurking in the background.

You want your boss to be on cc so that he can't then say that you sent something to the client and that he had no oversight over your work. It's all about CYA.

So make sure that the partner and other higher-ups are definitely on cc, whether they like it or not.

❊ ❊ ❊

When actually pitching for new work, you'll be surprised at what actually is acceptable. What would normally be considered guff, is now your best friend in clinching the deal.

Consider this hypothetical scenario:

Client: "Why should I hire you?"

Consultant: "What is it that you want? (Momentary pause for dramatic effect.) I'll tell you what. It's recognition. Recognition that you've worked mighty hard to bring yourself up to this esteemed position, all the while managing talented and dedicated staff members under your wing. Recognition that you guys are ahead of the pack and that you can't even see your competitors in the rear-view mirror. Recognition, as your website states, that you're world-leader in your segment and that you guys proactively look for challenging problems, find the leading-edge solutions to these problems, provide incisive insights into your customers' problems and drive change in a fast-changing industry that is replete with turmoil and upheaval, yet filled with opportunity if you know where to look and where to find it. We see yourselves as industry leaders and want to align ourselves to you. We're here to help you with your journey. Not just doing. Imagining."

Now try and tell me that you can't see yourself buying consulting services from me.

✿ ✿ ✿

The important point is to say lots without saying anything at all really. Consider the following example extracted from my book 'The Right Trajectory' which satirised a junior consultant's career path.

I decide to get this party started.

"Thank you all for your time today. I appreciate that you're all busy, so I will make this short and punchy. Of course, please feel free to ask questions along the way."

Starters done with, it was time for the main course.

"Let's start off by questioning your current strategy. Are you in the right vertical? Do you have the resources to meet the ever-changing landscape? More importantly, are you on the right trajectory?"

I let the silence linger for a moment as I take a breather. I look into the audience to get a feel for their emotions before I continue. I can see fear writ plainly on their faces. It's either the fear of me announcing redundancies or the fear of not wanting to call me out openly for my management consultant garbage. I don't know which fear was worse.

"You have this unique opportunity to seize the moment. Allow me to paint the picture for a moment. What you need now in your organisation is some blue-sky thinking to get the most operational efficiency. You can only do that if you had a bird's-eye view of the company and its operations. That's what we're here for."

I sense the fear levels rising in the room and people are beginning to fidget now.

I march on.

"As you scope the land ahead, you have to ask yourself some fundamental questions: are you in the b2b or b2c space? What domains do you want to dominate? Will everyone in the organisation be able to deliver this succinct corporate strategy in a 60-second elevator pitch *if the CEO happens to jump in at the same time?"*

People look positively mortified now. No one bargained for making a summary of their company's business strategy to their CEO. That too, in front of everyone else. Public speaking was bad enough for most people. But in a confined space and in front of their CEO? Come on, why do you want to scare someone like that?

"It's now time to open the kimono and look at what this changing landscape means for everyone concerned. We did a deep dive into the finance department and we've come up with a straw man argument as to why your current structure may or may not be optimal for your future plans. This, of course, is dependant on whether your senior management team seizes the opportunities presented to it and whether it wants to really bite the ass off the bear."

Another pause for added effect, before continuing.

"The main thing to keep in mind is that there are so many low-hanging fruits that one can leverage. There is so much potential for improvement that the opportunities are, literally, limitless."

[...]

"As I was saying, there's the immense opportunity for carpe diem, or to seize the day, as there is going to be a paradigm shift in the industry ahead. As I'm sure you're well aware, there's been a sea change in the industry of late and the regulator is getting more active in this space. The last thing you want is to lose sight of the ball, as your go-to-market strategy was not up to snuff and you're not on the same page as everyone else around."

More looks of fear (or is it dread now?) as no one wants to be left behind or be targeted by the regulator.

"So the question you really need to wrap your head around now is this: do you want to hit the ground running and close the loop when you may be thinking of staff alignment to job specs? More importantly, does this meet your organisation's sniff test? Will you be able to buck the trend and scope out the landscape in the face of ever-shifting sands under your feet?

Another pause before I wrap up this segment of the presentation.

"I suspect you're right. In fact, I suspect that you'd find the truth much closer to home than you'd think. After all, you don't want to end up boiling the ocean in your quest for something that you'll inevitably circle back to."

On and on and on I drone, using more jargon than any reasonable person can stand.

At the end of the 90-minute presentation, the participants are clearly exhausted in spite of just being seated on their asses. No, they're tired *because their mind is spinning from all that they've just heard.*

This was not the first consultant's presentation they've heard and you can bet your bottom dollar that it won't be their last.

Obviously, that was a work of fiction and exaggerated for comedic effect, but don't be surprised if real life in consulting is not that much farther away from fiction. You'll find your lingo changing as time goes by and, before you know it, your dreams will be fill with 60-second elevator pitches, b2b or b2c verticals and opening the kinono. You've been warned.

❄ ❄ ❄

Inventing Work

You'll frequently come across situations where your employer has recently been on a hiring rampage and now the chickens are coming home to roost. After all the grand plans of double-digit growth and the expectations of explosion in consulting services with the uptake in the economy, you may see the opposite.

Clients are spending less, using a novel technique of using their handsomely-paid, internal staff to do much of their work, much to the horror of the consulting industry. (I hesitate to call it a profession as that would imply that there is some sort of code of ethics or higher creed to serve.) Also, for the few projects that clients are willing to bring consultants in, they are now negotiating fees like never before and you will have to sell services at, relatively speaking, rock-bottom rates. Couple this with a higher cost base for the consultants (due to the now larger pool of employees) and you are now facing a serious hit to your margins.

Your management can probably ride these rough seas for a few months, probably a year if they play their cards right. But if it continues any longer than that, it means that the partners will have less money to spends on lavish mansions in the countryside, expensive holidays and overpriced dinners. So, a walk in the park, then.

A smart partner, to use the industry lingo, would have 'scanned the horizon' and seen the 'stormy seas ahead', but if it's one thing you can expect from consultants, it's that they never take their own advice.

Instead of making redundancies and focusing on higher-margin, niche services, they will have gone in the opposite direction by doubling your department's workforce in the last 18 months and selling services that your firm would have once turned your noses up to.

You could make the argument that you're still winning multi-million pound contracts, which is true, but that hides the fact that you now have massive costs, increased competition and more aggressive clients. Clients have you where they want you and they know it. What's worse is that your management knows it, too, and is going along for the ride. They have no option; they have to. They throw in all sorts of project freebies, lavish meals and glossy reports. Anything to retain clients and have them spend the tiniest morsel of their ever-shrinking budgets.

❀ ❀ ❀

Alas, don't fret for consultants. Before you grab a tissue and dab your eyes thinking about the plight of these poor souls, think again. They've been in the game so long now, that they get into 'action mode' before long.

When businesses and economies have downturns (as they inevitably will), the smart consultant knows that in order to get this client to part with their wallet, he needs to identify something of value. Something that can help the client save money.

The smarter consultant (which you, naturally, consider yourself to be) has a better trick. He invents a totally new problem and, mysteriously, shows up to solve it.

This is one of the oldest tricks in the book, but also one of the most reliable. After all, what good would a consultant be if he could not find a way to keep himself in perpetual employment?

It is a very simple and, at times, glamorous scheme. While clients are busy doing whatever it is they do best, you spot 'an opportunity for improvement' or, better yet, 'a strategic threat to their business model'. It's not enough to invent these problems. You have to give them a dose of respectability and seriousness by using hard-to-decipher and meaningless jargon.

So, before long, you will work with your marketing department to put out magazine articles, host industry conferences and print brochures in large numbers to put the word out. The client goes from one day enjoying his cappuccino on his 07:34 from Guildford to London Waterloo, to now worrying about the 'perilous state of the industry', 'increasing cost pressures', 'more regulatory intervention', 'currency headwinds' and how household budgets are 'stretched beyond capacity'. All this before the client has even had a chance to enjoy his recently-purchased, onboard chocolate croissant.

When said client gets off the train, he picks up a copy of the free business newspaper, which has 'exclusive interviews' with partners in your firm where they are portrayed as 'industry experts' and 'thought leaders'. You then reinforce the message that the client is dumb, he knows nothing and is nothing without you. He arrives in his office, launches his email program where you bombard him with invitations to your free seminars on how he can 'keep up to date on tailwinds driving the industry' or how he can benefit from your 'desire to help clients define their capital agenda and drive competitive advantage'.

He then attends this session, where he is incessantly bombarded with messages such as 'how the landscape has rapidly shifted', how 'confidence levels have held in spite of receding asset strength', the 'ever-changing dynamic in the hunt for yield', the need to 'counter the dent of profit expectations' but not before 'quashing volatility and returning to pre-crisis levels along the risk-adjusted curve of stability in the face of rapid consolidation in increasingly fragmented markets'.

I kid you not.

The poor sod had no chance of survival before he even ordered his cappuccino earlier that morning. He is powerless against the might of the marketing department of a top-tier consulting firm. He'd have to be a fool to even entertain the notion of putting up a fight against you.

* * *

Staff Resignations

If you're an old hand at the consulting game, you'll come to expect a raft of resignations and finding yourself a bit short-staffed on projects.

This is far from surprising. The partners went and promised a whole lot of people promotions, but very few were forthcoming. No surprise that these employees decided to take their business elsewhere. This is par for the course in a consulting firm. The two or three months after promotions were announced are always punctuated with tantrums, threats of resignations, pay hikes and/or hastily-announced promotions or actual staff resignations.

It is so regular that the post-promotion period is terrible for your health. You'd find your inbox bulging at its space-allocated seams with invitations for leaving drinks, one last 'catch up' before staff members leave and farewell emails with promises to 'keep in touch', invitations to 'connect on LinkedIn' and vague tales of how they are leaving in spite of the 'excellent work atmosphere', 'outstanding colleagues' and 'invaluable experience'. Must be something in the water that drove them away, then.

So, in many ways, this should not be a surprise to you and you should take it in your stride. You had to if you were on the top of your game. Anything else and you'd look like an amateur.

❋ ❋ ❋

As they say on London's various transport systems, "All change, please." Don't worry, no one is moving around. But you're running short of skilled staff members on other projects and you're facing pressure to allocate them elsewhere. Genuinely skilled staff members are always a short commodity in consulting firms. If for no other reason, poor career management and unfulfilled promises litter one's career path here and you either had to be a shrewd political operator to survive here or you became someone else's lunch.

Most normal people's needs boil down to three basic requirements: to work in a place where they are paid a fair wage; have colleagues that are friendly; and, an office that is not too far to get to.

Given the simple list above, it would seem an easy thing to do. Alas, consulting firms are anything but normal and this list is asking for too much. They perpetually underpay you compared to what you could be earning working at clients' offices instead; you have psychopaths and backstabbers for colleagues (and that's just the girls at reception); and, you don't have a fixed location. One week you're in vibrant, exciting London, the next, you're in some drab back office in Leicester. When you are at 'home base', you don't even have a desk to call our own. Sure, being mobile when you're in your twenties sounds like a great gig; think of it as a sort of paid backpacking jaunt. But when you're in your thirties and forties and your body is not as nimble as it used to be (especially if you're a woman and have given birth to children), this suddenly seems a poor way to waste one's life.

To paraphrase Lord Alfred Tennyson's poem The Brook: For resignations come and resignations may go, but the consulting firm goes on forever.

❈ ❈ ❈

Bait N' Switch

Ah, yes, The old 'Bait N' Switch'. A consultant's classic trick.

It's where you get some of the more experienced managers on the job to start off with and then slowly transition them out one by one when they've settled in. Later on, there will be a chance to train up some of the juniors and leave them running the show.

Let me illustrate by way of an example.

❊ ❊ ❊

Imagine you bought a new computer. You paid top dollar for it and are happy with its performance. One month in, the vendor calls you and says that he's giving you a free printer to go with it. Of course, you're chuffed to bits. You say, "Yes, please."

A few weeks roll by and then the vendor calls again. This time, he sends you a free keyboard, but it's not as fancy as the one you got included originally. But, it's free, so where's the harm?

Again, a few weeks roll by and then you get a new monitor. Okay, it's a bit smaller and not as high resolution as the one bundled originally, but, hey, it's free! You say 'okay' and now you have a backup monitor if something should ever go wrong.

This goes on and on, over the next few weeks and, before long, you have extras for everything. This is when the fun begins.

Now, the vendor calls in to ask to borrow back the printer, 'just for a few days'. You instinctively want to say 'no' but you did get it free, after all. And he only wants to borrow it, so there should be no harm. You reluctantly say 'okay' and now you have no printer.

A few days later, he calls again, this time asking if he can borrow the original keyboard he supplied. You, after all, have the second one he sent over previously, so this is no big deal. And, he's only borrowing it, so it's only a temporary situation. What could go wrong?

On and on he goes, 'borrowing' part after original part, leaving you with all the inferior substitutes. After a while, you finally realise that you're the victim of a very fancy bait n' switch operation.

Welcome to the life of a consultant.

Since there's only a limited resource in our firms (i.e., genuinely smart workers), there's only so many projects they can work on. So you engineer a solution that works. Well, one that works for you at least. Who cares about the client?

You bring in our A-team to begin with. You'll supply the best and brightest, the ones who have genuine industry experience and who actually know what they're talking about. They will come from a broad range of backgrounds, having worked in the industry (but now, bizarrely, want to work at a consulting firm to 'broaden their experience'), maybe they did some time at the regulator's office (which they left before they became 'institutionalised') or they worked up the ranks in the consulting firm itself (because they were too stupid to move elsewhere until they realised it was too late).

For the first week, or the first month if it's a longer-term project, the A-team will be on-site. Laptops all fired up, notepads at hand and the senior ones with Mont Blanc pens ready to be flashed out, even if it's a note to remind you about the meeting that's in your calendar.

Then, that's when the magic begins. The senior manager on the project will bring in a total newbie. Usually a graduate, this person is bright, but knows very little. So why would a client pay for this cretin? They don't. At first.

The senior manager will usually say something along the lines of, "This is Peter. He's our newest recruit and we thought that what better way to expose him to the work than to have him at our best client, working on the most interesting projects. What's that? Oh no, we won't be charging you for his. He'll only be a mute spectator at meetings and will have no major role to play in the final deliverables. Yes, no cost to you. We'll swallow his training costs. After all, it's how we make sure our people have the breadth of experience to bear on projects — by exposing them to the best in the industry! Oh, don't be so shy. I can confidently state that from my many years of experience, you guys are easily in the upper quartile. With this project, you'll easily be in the top decile. Oh, you're very welcome. The pleasure is all ours."

Sounds fair enough, I hear you say. Maybe it is; maybe it isn't. Let's progress.

A week (or month) rolls by and now Sally, the top manager on your project will be joined by Evan. You know, just to speed things along. "No, don't worry, we're still within budget and if costs were to escalate, we'd swallow it. Oh, you're very welcome."

Another week/month and you've supplemented another three or four other positions. This time, however, you decide to take Sally off the project. After all, Evan has been sharing her responsibilities all this time and it makes sense for him to take on the role full-time. "What's that? No, of course, there are no cost implications to you. Oh, you're very welcome."

A few more weeks/months and this time, you pull out all the other original staff members and leave their dud replacements behind. In the span of a few weeks/months, you now have a totally new team and the client's staff members have to do yet another round of hand-holding, explaining and being patient with your new arrivals. The junior staff members at the client know the game, but are powerless to stop it. The senior ones are too busy being wined and dined by your partners to know what's going on. Besides, you send them a nice, shiny and colourful 'status report' ever so often with its RAG (Red, Amber, Green) status symbols and complicated Gantt charts that no one seems to really understand or care about.

By now, Peter, our original newbie, is actually the most experienced one on the project. Of course, he's the cheapest one too, having worked for free all these months. The senior manager then turns to the client and suggests that Peter take on more responsibilities as he's become very experienced in a short period of time and is well-known by the client's staff members. Another week or month in and Peter is now pretty much running the show, acting as a good number two to the original number two (i.e., the senior manager). An assistant to the assistant, as it were. What's more, Peter's charge-out rates are cheaper, so everyone is a winner. "What's that? Oh, you're very welcome."

You now have a project with either lesser-experienced consultants or, worse yet, total duds. The only one who actually knows what the hell is going on is a 23-year old graduate who started working only six months back. But you have nice reports landing up in your inbox every week, a regular conference call (that you can initiate from home in your PJs) and a top brand name for the client to show his boss or regulator when he gets asked why this year's Christmas party budget is smaller than ever before.

Where are the original consultants you pulled off this project? Well, they're at other clients' sites, on new projects, settling down, until it's time to pull the old switcheroo again.

Rinse and repeat.

"What's that? Oh, you're very welcome."

Get this trick right and your projects
should be on time and on budget forever.

❁ ❁ ❁

Utilisation

A consulting firm has employees over by a barrel and the partners know it. One of the metrics in your annual performance appraisal is your 'utilisation'. You see, employees are the new assets in the knowledge economy and, just like regular assets, they needed to be 'utilised' or 'sweated'. More likely, they are treated like workhorses with the whip constantly behind them.

Once a week, like clockwork, an email will come out from the operations team detailing your 'utilisation'. This is a very easy-to-calculate statistic, but probably the most deadly for management to wield. It was nothing more than a percentage of the time worked on projects ("chargeable hours") to hours available in a week. For example, there are 35 hours in a week (nominally, at seven hours a day) and if you worked for 28 (four days' worth) on a particular project, you'd have 80% utilisation. Simple to calculate, but the most potent one to club employees with.

Firstly, this report detailing everyone's productivity in the past week is sent out to the whole department. This is, effectively, a name and shame practice. The ones on top of the leagues have nothing to worry about, but the ones at the lower half had better get their act together, and soon. At one glance, you knew who the 'productive' ones were and who the slackers were. What's worse is that, if for some reason your project did not start this week and you had nothing else to do, you'd be at the bottom of the leagues on next week's report and would remain there, at least until you were able to get your project going. So even a temporary blip in productivity can send you into cold sweats and induce panic attacks.

This practice is brutal and ensures that everyone plays ball and is not goofing off. At least, not for too long. The problem arises when your firm is now positively overstaffed and, as I'd mentioned before, clients are preferring to do projects in-house. So you now have staff members fighting to pick scraps off the table in the quest to be at least in the middle leagues of the table. Anything but in the bottom quartile, which feels more like purgatory as the months go by.

❊ ❊ ❊

Client Types

The main honchos:
If you're lucky, you'll get the easy-going client who is the one that's going to hire you. They're gullible, easily to part from their money and keen to maintain an image with their bosses, so will lap up whatever you have to say.

The sharp number twos:
The second in command is, quite frequently, the one you'll need to watch out for. Just five minutes into the conversation with him and you'll pick up that he's the actual brains behind the operations and that his boss has either slept her way to the top or is there to tick some 'diversity' box. Seems unfair, but that's life. Shit happens.

It's the sharp number twos that you should worry about. These guys have a pleasant demeanour but, under it, hide a ferociously astute mind and they can cut through all the bullshit, especially when they're handing over millions of pounds to consultants. If you're a consultant who's good at his game, you'll come to like these chaps as they keep you on your toes and genuinely respect you when you can reveal something to them that they did not previously know.

None the less, don't let your guard down with these number twos. He will keep checking in whenever your staff members are on-site and likes to pepper them with questions. Luckily, you will have anticipated this and briefed the guys on the job. Train them on what to say (lots, without very much in the way of substance), what to focus on (not giving any definitive opinion) and what to avoid (any criticism of the client, even if it's a glaringly obvious fault).

❊ ❊ ❊

So, why do I like the head honchos? For the same reason men love slappers at the bar. They're just easier and don't make you jump through all these hoops. Sure, the intelligent ones can provide you intellectual fodder on a languid Sunday afternoon, but when you're out on a Saturday night, you just want to bust a nut with the nearest thing that has a pulse.

As a senior manager, you're typically handling multiple projects on the go and have little time, or patience, for clients who like to challenge you on every single remark you make or observation you bring to their notice. You'd much rather spew some garbage, have the client lap it up and collect the cheque without passing through jail.

Choose your clients carefully. A dumb and gullible one that you've managed to keep happy is a definite repeat customer, while a share cookie will sniff you out immediately and it'll be a struggle to finish the project, least of all think of project extensions or repeat business.

❊ ❊ ❊

Alas, do not get too close to your clients and do not let sentiment rule over your senses.

The show must go on. You've got bills to pay, too, and being sentimental isn't going to pay them.

So, you learn to build up this thick layer of skin and pick up tricks of subterfuge to muddle along and get the results you need. Once your report is delivered, it's time for your boys and girls to pack up and ship out and stay away from the inevitable 'kaboom' that's bound to make its way to the client's management team if your report says that they're anything but stellar.

If you're the client, when the shit hits the fan, the consultants you hired are the last ones to be found around. Here today, gone tomorrow. They borrowed your watch to tell you the time, but they've now disappeared while you were still reeling from the magic trick.

❀ ❀ ❀

Client Tricks

Before you get all teary-eyed for your clients and think that all consultants are scum, it's not all sunshine and roses on the client's side.

As I alluded to before, sometimes you're just hired for the brand you bring. It's not the work you do, the people you put on the job or the actual results you deliver. Many a time, middle- and even senior-level management in companies are extremely insecure about their positions. (Well, who wouldn't be if you were vastly overpaid, did very little and were probably underqualified?) In many cases, your career or position in a firm can be bolstered, or downright saved, if you get a report from a big-name consulting firm saying that it has reviewed your systems and controls and everything is, for the most part, hunky-dory. Well, apart from a few minor recommendations for improvement, of course, as no one is perfect.

Another factor to take into account is the concept of scope creep. This is when a client hires you to do A, B and C, but then adds X, Y and Z to the list after you've signed the contract and land on-site. This is one of the more insidious client practices as consultants are now in the position of a bait n' switch themselves and may end up working more than anticipated on this 'one last thing' the client wants to add to the list of deliverables. It's one thing to ask your electrician to look at the door handle while he's there, but it's another to ask him to do the gas check. It may be something he's unqualified for or, worse, underinsured for in case something goes wrong horribly wrong. It's similar in the consulting world where they treat additional client requests with a very skeptical eye. If nothing else, they'd like to be compensated for it and are happy to do it as long as clients are willing to pay extra. After all, no one like to work for free when he's got bills to pay. More importantly, if there's a screw up somewhere down the line, this 'small freebie' is now an insurance and legal liability for the consulting firm.

Then there's the legal (and personal) minefield of job offers to join the 'dark side' i.e., join the client as an employee. A consultant's comparatively meagre pay can only pay for so many rounds of drinks at the bar, so do not underestimate the temptation of a massive pay hike by joining a client and bidding adieu to a consultant's life. The partners in consulting firms hate this and usually have clauses specifically banning poaching of their employees, but these clauses are rarely enforced. Especially, when clients dangle the carrot of future work in front of the partners' eyes.

What if I ask the aforementioned electrician to send his invoice after he's done and then sit on his bill? Even if he chases me with phone calls, emails or text messages, I can pay him whenever (or if) I want to, as these services have been rendered and I am now in the position of power. Well, it's the same for consultants, with the notable exception of the electrician being able to sue you in a court of law. Consultants can, technically speaking, go down that route too, but they are too conservative an industry for that. After all, when was the last time you hear of an accountant, lawyer or white-shoe consultant suing their client? Probably once in a blue moon. It's a professional no-no and they go to great lengths to avoid the negative publicity that will invariable follow such cases. They'd prefer to take a hit to their profits and never work with the client again rather than sue in court. Of course, it's another matter that the client invariably comes crawling back on his hands and knees when he needs help again or his regulator is breathing fire up his ass. Magically, all outstanding bills are paid, the consultant acts as if nothing ever happened and they go back to holding hands and singing Kumbaya.

Of course, the consultant can always take their revenge on such clients such as billing them their full, undiscounted rates when clients come back begging for help. The consultant knows that he is in the position of power and that the client has to cough up.

A consultant's personal favourite, though, is bidding low and charging high. They come in with a very low, but not incredulous, bid and, once in, they take every opportunity to milk the client for extras and charge for the most basic of stuff, including printouts and postage charges. Invariably, such contracts end up costing two to three times the original estimate as the original bid was a sham to begin with, but the client has no choice now since he's committed to the project and can't afford to re-tender and go through all that pain again. They just have to grin and bear it while they bend over.

Someone once said somewhere that 'All's fair in love and war'. That is certainly the case with sometimes bumbling, sometimes wily clients and their sometimes pitiful, sometimes scheming consultants.

❋ ❋ ❋

Part III: Getting Out

Deciding to Leave

At some point, life in consulting will get to you — the colleagues, the travel, the clients, the office politics, the lack of promotion opportunities, the loneliness, or a whole host of other factors.

It happens to everybody (apart from those that made partner, that is, as they're all in) and now's the time to decide if you're ready to pull the trigger and jump ship.

The colleagues you work with may be idiots. Sure, there are some true gems around, but such guys are few and far between and, unfortunately, don't last long in places like this. In this place, you either make lunch of others or prepare to become someone else's lunch yourself.

Worse still, you may no longer recognise yourself in the mirror when you shave every morning. You may recall earlier thoughts of consulting being a respectable job and paying good money. A solid middle-class one at that. Though the money part of that dream was sorely missing in the earlier part of your consulting career, it will pick up once you move on up the ranks. But that just means more deadlines and more stress to accompany the money. So, it does come at a price.

You may also feel burdened by the expectations of friends and relatives. What started out as an optimistic, if naive, view of the modern workplace has changed you into a dark and brooding figure at get-togethers. You now only think of ways of escaping the rat race and making a clean break. But no one else seems to understand you.

"Why do you want to be so rash? Why give up all that you've worked for? What will you do if you quit?"

These are the sorts of questions people will lobby at you whenever you speak to near and dear ones about this dull, aching throb in your soul.

The decision to leave it all behind and to move on to a new job hits everyone in their consulting career at one point or another. You may delay it, but never fully escape it.

After all, what's the point of looking back at your life when you're 80 years old and on your deathbed, but then just wishing you'd done more in life. I had come across this quote from Mark Twain once and it is helpful to keep in mind when you decide to quit and move to newer pastures:

"Twenty years from now you will be more disappointed by the things that you didn't do than by the ones you did. So throw off the bowlines. Sail away from the safe harbour. Catch the trade winds in your sails. Explore. Dream. Discover."

❈ ❈ ❈

Farewell Email

It's your last day of work. You're ready to say goodbye to everything and to start again. For once in your life, you do not have to worry about calendar entries reminding you of some client office you're meant to be at, reports to be issued, presentations to be given, spreadsheets to be filled in, expense reports to be mailed or performance reviews to be done.

Before you switch off your laptop for the last time and hand it back in, think about sending a farewell email. It is something that many are usually loathe to receive in their inbox, but if you feel it seems appropriate, do so. Just be sure to keep it short and brief.

✵ ✵ ✵

Dear Colleagues

As you may have heard, I have decided to leave to pursue other career opportunities.

I wish to thank you all for the invaluable experience as I believe that it has all made me a better professional. I will sorely miss the excellent work atmosphere and outstanding colleagues.

I wish you the best in all your future endeavours and hope you find happiness in whatever you choose to do.

I'd love to keep in touch. Here are my details:
Email
Phone
LinkedIn

I'm organising leaving drinks this Thursday, so I hope to see you all for one last farewell there!

Regards
Former Consultant

❊ ❊ ❊

Wrapping Up

If you recall a previous chapter, I said that drinking is a big part of the work culture here. Keeping in line with that, be sure to organise one last leaving drinks session on your last day at work or, if leaving mid-week, on the Thursday or Friday before. People will somehow remember you later in life for the leaving drinks rather than the 90 hours a week you worked on their projects.

That's consulting for you!

❉ ❉ ❉

I hope you now have a better understanding of the world of consulting and its various intricacies. If you decide to go in, I wish you all the best! If you decide it's not for you or are already in and now looking to leave, I hope you catch the wind in your sails and explore new worlds.

If you liked this book, you may wish to consider reading 'The Right Trajectory' which is a satirical tale of a consultant's career at a prestigious, big-name firm. You'll recognise a lot of what has been said here, but this book is a fun way of absorbing it all in! Details are at the end of this book.

< < < < The End > > > >

Bibliography

1. 5 Job Interview Questions That Mean You're Not Getting Hired…And One That Means You Are
http://bit.ly/11THzSx

2. It's OK – the Big Four still seem to be hiring thousands of people
http://bit.ly/1ziSnog

3. Good reasons to tolerate lower paid work as a consultant in the Big Four (read the comments too)
http://bit.ly/1zPXlsS

4. The truth about Big 4 employees, busy season, and fagony
http://exm.nr/12temyP

5. PwC, Deloitte, E&Y, and KPMG: Big 4 employees modern indentured servants
http://exm.nr/1wr1LZy

6. Office Space
http://bit.ly/1vmBWs9

7. The corporate guff award goes to...
http://bbc.in/1HZwIaP

8. Business jargon: Squaring the circle
http://bbc.in/1pTdPQT

9. Op-Ed: Microsoft layoff e-mail typifies inhuman corporate insensitivity
http://bit.ly/1tMk30p
http://bit.ly/1zPY5xU

10. Why everyone is so "shocked" about the UK passport fiasco
http://bit.ly/1BdePDm

11. McKinsey, the Insider Trading Scandal, and the Problems With Consulting
http://bit.ly/1yhibPz

12. Get Connected! GE's Equipment Insight Solution Enables New Industrial Internet Service Offering
http://yhoo.it/1vNh8sl

13. The dirty tricks clients play
http://tek.io/1vNhbED

14. Don't play dirty consultant tricks
http://tek.io/1pTeEJr

15. 7 dirty consultant tricks (and how to avoid them)
http://bit.ly/1pTeKRj

16. Modern Workplaces Demand A High Price For Promotion
http://bit.ly/1yOn72n

17. The Management Consulting Lingo Dictionary
http://bit.ly/1tE0f01

18. EY Q2 2014 Analysis of profit warnings, Issued by UK quoted companies (PDF)
http://bit.ly/1BdfiFC

Contact Details

Did you enjoy the book? If so, please leave a review on Amazon's website — it really helps! Thanks!

Want to keep in touch?
Email: john.kumar@sent.as
Twitter: @JuanKumario

By the Same Author

The Right Trajectory

Quick! When I mention the name of a
top-tier professional services firm, what
do you think of?

Plush offices, great colleagues, prestigious
jobs?

Well, what if I told you it actually
epitomised incompetence, bureaucracy,
poisonous office politics and sex, all
thrown in together?

Surprised? Well, read on for one man's
inside story on how these firms really
work, the unhinged people you'll come
across and what you can do to protect

yourself against the insanity of such environments.

Available from Amazon both in print and ebook versions:
US: http://amzn.to/1zB5W6b
UK: http://amzn.to/1GZNXY8

By the Same Author

Exact Change Only

A bus driver, a pensioner, an advertising executive, a shop manager, a plumber, a banker, a nanny, a school teacher and a young man. All travelling on Bus number 59 in London. Will they reach their final destination?

This is a story about their lives.

Available from Amazon both in print and ebook versions:
US
Print: http://amzn.to/1zKT7R8
Ebook: http://amzn.to/1jTmO11

UK
Print: http://amzn.to/1CDVVnM

ebook: http://amzn.to/1B5NKil

Notes

Notes

Notes